Facilitating Change to Reach All Generations

Endorsements

"Pastor Wickham's book goes beyond mere description of generational differences to tackle the extraordinary challenges for contemporary chur-ches to build God's Kingdom in a secular, humanistic culture. He offers sound, Bible-based wisdom for changing church culture in order to disciple all generations."

—**Dr. Kristin D. Wilson**
Church of God in Christ Ministries, local Director on Board of Trustees and Director of Auxiliary Leader Training
St. Paul Church of God in Christ, Rockford, IL

"Dr. Jim Wickham's signature exploration and observed case study in facilitating change is a road atlas and thought-provoking debut. Sections One and Two are worth the price of admission! His breakdown of the generations from Traditionalists to Gen Zs is resonant with meaning, capturing the essence of an adventurous journey to church health. Jim's approach allows for an arresting hybrid for multiple genres of church culture to find brilliant insight and great depth for the preparing of something remarkable.

—**Dr. Joseph S. Girdler**
Superintendent, Kentucky Assemblies of God, Crestwood, KY
Author of: *A Christian's Pilgrimage: Israel; Setting the Atmosphere for the Day of Worship I and II; Redemptive Missiology in Pneumatic Context;* and *Keys to the Apostolic and Prophetic: Embracing the Authentic ~ Avoiding the Bizarre.*

"The issues leading multigenerational churches are complex. We need definite solutions and answers that adequately address the tensions in love. A church is accountable to nurture its culture within the church, so it welcomes and receives all generations. Dr. Wickham gives a biblically grounded and solutions-oriented approach to leading in a way that embraces younger generations. This book reflects his long-term pastoral experience and excellent education. I appreciate how he carefully addresses challenges facing each generation within our culture in order to demon-strate God's plan of an intergenerational Church. This book will serve the

Church's multiplication efforts well as it seeks to reach all generations."

—**Dr. Mike McCrary**
National Director of Partnerships,
Church Multiplication Network of the Assemblies of God
Springfield, MO

"The church in America is facing increasing challenges to stay relevant in an aggressive post-Christian culture. Without losing the foundational truths of the gospel, we have to be able to look future generations in the eye and offer a message that declares that Jesus is love and still in the life transfor-mational business today. We have to go beyond the lights and smoke and get to some real heart issues.

In his book *Facilitating Change to Reach All Generations*, Dr. James Wickham sheds light on some of the challenges the church is facing and offers insight as to how to move forward. The book is built solidly on a theology of culture and shows us why it is important for church leaders to think through the issues before moving too quickly to execute strategies. It takes time to listen and learn, but patience and persistence are required in order to understand different world views.

I have known Dr. James for many years now. He is a pastor who cares deeply for the church and its desire to relate to all generations, current and future. I am confident you will find this book a helpful resource for you and your church leadership.

—**Dr. Keith G. Edwards**
Executive Regional Presbyter, Potomac Ministry Network of the AG,
Lead Pastor of Centerpointe Church, Fairfax, VA

Facilitating **Change** to Reach All **Generations**

James W. Wickham

**Foreword by
Mark Lehmann**

Facilitating
Change to Reach
All Generations

Copyright © 2020. All rights reserved. Except for brief quotations in critical publications or reviews, no part of this book may be reproduced in any manner without prior written permission from the publisher.

ISBN: 978-1-7352175-0-5

Facilitating Change to Reach All Generations by James W. Wickham; foreword by Mark Lehmann.
Includes bibliographical references.
Manufactured in the U.S.A.

The Holy Bible, New International Version, copyright 1986, Holman Bible Publishers, by Broadman & Holman Publishers. Nashville, TN. Used by permission. All rights reserved.

Dedication

*Dedicated to Isla,
who has been my wife for over forty-one years.*

*I appreciate your love and support
more than you will ever know.*

Table of Contents

Foreword	xiii
Preface	xv
Acknowledgments	xvii
Introduction	xix
SECTION ONE	1
1 The Beginning of God's Cultural Project	3
2 A Cultural Responsibility	21
3 Jesus, Culture Maker	29
4 Beyond Pentecost and Cultural Boundaries	39
SECTION TWO	47
5 Understanding Culture	51
6 Understanding the Generations	59
7 Barriers or Connectors?	77
SECTION THREE	83
8 Seminar Agenda and Session Overview	85
9 Facilitator's Guide	93
10 Assessing Your Teaching	171
11 Benefits to Your Ministry	183
12 Final Reflections	185
About the Author	191
Endnotes	193

Foreword

Ministry moves at the speed of change. Once, it seemed that all a church had to do was obtain a building, get a pastor, and put a sign out in front. People would just come, stay, and grow together with little effort. That, of course, is a simplistic view, and by anyone's assessment, those days of simpler church ministry are long gone.

Now we feel the constant tug of so many options for each genera-tion in the church, and at the same time we hear so many differing opinions as to how a church should function relating to keeping younger and older generations on the same page. We face a huge challenge. How do we teach people on different frequencies, at different ages, and at different stages across the intergenerational spectrum, what church life should be like?

This question remains vital, not only for the health of a local church but for the long-term future and effectiveness of the Church of Jesus globally. This crisis needs a solution. Questions need clear answers and responses that are not mere platitudes but practical and effective.

Recent statistics say that people of all ages are abandoning church at record levels. That is why the book you are about to read is so impor-tant for all of us. How do we engage the ministry of Jesus in His church across generational lines? If we are serious about affecting our church, our community, our nation, and the world, we must desire to see change, commit to implementing it, and determine to persevere in our efforts.

This is why I feel so excited for what you are about to experience. Dr. Jim Wickham addresses these vital questions in His work, *Facilitating Change to Reach all Generations*. I have had the privilege of being connected to Jim in ministry for more than two decades. During that time, I have observed his obvious passion for people and the church he loves. His life experience as a church planter, community leader, and long-term pastor qualifies Jim not only to give insights, but to give you practical solutions in pastoring a multi-generational church. For more than thirty years, Pastor Jim has lived out the values you will read about in the pages that follow.

In the adventure you are about to take, you will see that facilitating change really begins with a cultural shift in the local church and with the church understanding that in order to accomplish the mission of the local church, they must be counterculture to that of the world around them. But how is that accomplished? And how can we take churches set in their ways and declining and allow the Holy Spirit to form a God-pleasing, life-giving culture for all generations to worship and minister effectively together? You are about to find out.

May God speak to you and your church in a profound way through the pages of this book. May you have God-given boldness to build and equip churches that celebrate the wonderful generational diversity of our Lord's Church. Let the journey begin!

Mark Lehmann
Cornerstone Church; Bowie, MD
Assistant Superintendent,
Potomac Ministry Network

Preface

This book has been in the making for over thirty-three years. The church my wife, Isla, and I pastor is a church plant. We did not move to Mechanicsville, Maryland community to plant a church. It was only after we settled in that the Lord began to speak to us that He wanted a church in this community—and so we planted Living Word Community Church in 1986. As Living Word began to grow, it was natural for us to connect with the various generations through the multiple ministries the church offered. That ability to connect with the different generations came due to the good working relationship between my youth pastor and myself. As we worked as a team to bridge that gap, the church grew vibrantly through strong youth, children's, and adult ministries.

The new millennium brought changes to society that presented significant challenges to Living Word. As American culture changed radically, the church was facing cultural challenges that were questioning its very existence and its methods for reaching the lost. These cultural changes began to cause a gap between the older and younger generations of the church. Concurrently, church leaders turned their attention more inward in order to build ministries, struggling to keep them strong with people willing to serve. As leaders continued to focus their attention inward, a large gap between the older and younger generations continued to widen. Cultural realities within society as well as leadership decisions within the local church each made bridging the gap between the generations at Living Word more difficult. Something had to be done.

This book describes the journey Living Word took in order to connect and reach all generations. Since this book was originally a project fulfilling a Doctor of Ministry degree requirement, it is limited in its scope and therefore does not claim to answer every question for every church. However, our journey described within

Facilitating Change to Reach All Generations

this book can serve as a model for your church as it addresses important issues for you to discuss and possible shifts you can make if your church is going to reach all generations.

I pray this book will inform, encourage, inspire, and challenge you and your congregation to make changes that can facilitate reaching the lost generations within your community. Blessings!

Acknowledgments

This book is the result of a project that was produced to meet requirements for fulfilling a Doctor of Ministry Degree. Several people were part of making that project a success, and each had such an important part to play in that process. However, transforming an academic assignment into a book that leaders and lay people could find helpful and practical for reaching all generations required another set of skills and help. I am humbled by the fact that others were so willing to help me in such an endeavor.

First, there were family members who encouraged me to transform this project into a book. They felt it addressed relevant issues with practical and helpful insights for the challenges they were facing every day. I am grateful for my children and their spouses who consistently encouraged me to move forward with this book. Thank you, Tracey and Terry Marshall, Reneé and David Lehmann, and Nathaniel and Jessica Wickham. I am thankful too for my wife, Isla, for her constant support. From the beginning of the project to this moment, she felt that this material offered helpful insights for those wanting to reach all generations.

Second, this book would not even be a reality if it were not for the help of Dr. Lois Olena. Not having the knowledge or the experience of ever writing a book myself, Dr. Olena assisted me in ways that made this experience considerably enjoyable. Her knowledge, experience, and wisdom of having written books before and helping others in such endeavors made this book a reality. Dr. Olena's skills in editing and formatting for publishing have been invaluable. Her attention to detail helped refine this work, assisting in making its message stronger and clearer.

Third, I had no clue about a design for a cover for such a book. I am very grateful for Dr. Doug Olena's creativity. He provided several presentations of design with different ideas for the cover. It was Doug's ability to capture the essence of the book in a design that hopefully will seize people's attention and stir their curiosity to want to read this book.

Finally, it is with a humble heart that I say thank you to my Lord and Savior Christ Jesus. If not for the support and assistance He provided throughout the entire project, I would not be writing this acknowledgement today.

I am extremely grateful for each one who has played an important part of this endeavor. Thank you!

Introduction

> If one wishes to distinguish leadership from management or administration, one can argue that leaders create and change culture, while management and administration act within culture.
> —Edgar H. Schein[1]

On July 13, 1986, Living Word Community Church held its first service with seventeen people in a two-car garage. My wife and I did not move to this community to plant a church. After the Lord directed us to settle in Mechanicsville, Maryland, He began to speak to us that He wanted a Pentecostal church in this community. From that humble beginning, the church has grown from one service to multiple services and ministries, relocated three times, undergone three major name changes, and experienced several traumatic challenges.

I serve as lead pastor with several part-time and full-time staff. The newer staff members are all young adults who have grown up in the church; one is the full-time worship/media pastor along with his wife, who serves as part-time youth director. The children's pastor and her husband serve part-time. Three staff serve part-time in the office and have worked with me from seventeen to over thirty years: executive secretary, the ministry administrator, and the treasurer/business manager. About eighty-six percent of the leaders in Living Word, including the office staff, are forty or older, and most of those (sixty-five percent) are over fifty.

Living Word has weekly services for the entire family. The services include inspiring and uplifting worship, challenging sermons with insightful Bible teaching, and age-specific ministries that fit all generations. In February 2018, we added an early Sunday morning service to help address the desire for an earlier but shorter service. The later service includes ministry to children, with nursery and toddler care provided. Also, the main service was adjusted to be sensitive toward people's schedules. The Wednesday night ministries include Royal Rangers, Girls Impact, youth service, nursery, and adult ministries with contemporary worship.

When my wife and I first arrived in this community, the area was rural with some large farms and a strong Amish community. Locals commute to Washington D.C., northern Virginia, and Baltimore for work. The main crop in the Mechanicsville area when my wife and I first moved here was tobacco, which has dramatically changed.

A strong military presence remains in the area with Andrews Air Force Base, along with other nearby military installations. Every change in political administration has brought with it shifting priorities concerning the size of the military. Since 2001, military installations around us, especially a naval base to the south, have grown, bringing a population increase in Mechanicsville and the surrounding areas. Though the area still has some farms and an Amish community, more people work for the government, do government contract work, or serve in the military. Diversity in the Mechanicsville area has also increased. Latinos now represent a rapidly growing ethnic group, a change from the county previously being predominately African American and White. Although there is this increase in the population and diversity, the area is still strongly Catholic.

Until 2008, Living Word had naturally connected with the various generations through the ministries of the church. At the time, the youth/assistant pastor and I worked together connecting the generations. The church grew vibrantly and had strong youth and children's ministries. Along with the growth, however, came personnel changes, and I began to focus on managing more than leading. That change in focus from leading to managing caused the leadership and myself to turn inward, losing our missional focus of making disciples. We were concerned about strengthening the ministries and striving to get adults involved in serving, and we missed the shift that was occurring.

Introduction

That shift dramatically increased after a change occurred with the youth pastor. As the church leadership turned more attention inward to build the ministries, a gap grew between the present church members and the younger generation. As time passed, the church began to struggle to keep ministries strong and to recruit people to serve, and the gap between the generations continued to widen. As Living Word became more internally focused, society also changed with the new millennium. In recent decades, the United States has radically changed, and Living Word needed to adjust its methods for reaching the lost.

Living Word Community Church needed a culture change, too, one that welcomes and supports new and younger people. Leaders provide the critical component for enacting this transformation. With the majority of its leaders forty and older, this required an intentional strategy to help them refocus on connecting with the next generations. Though the leaders at Living Word do reach out and welcome new people, a problem persisted with leaders having to multitask and serve in multiple positions. Newer congregants were not taking ownership, nor becoming involved in serving. The original strategy for Living Word never intended for leaders to have to multitask in multiple ministry positions.

Though numerous problems and challenges called for my attention, I wanted to primarily walk with the leadership of Living Word through a process of refocusing missionally on developing a culture that intentionally includes and reaches all generations. I firmly believed that leaders must connect with the younger generations and help them better engage in the ministries of Living Word.

Thus, I purposed to train the leaders and influencers of Living Word about the differences between the generations, different kinds of people, and cultural changes in America. I decided to center my teaching on four main objectives: (1) to help leaders and influencers understand the challenges faced in reaching the generations, (2) to help them understand culture and its effect on everyone, including the church, (3) to provide insight regarding God's plan of a counterculture, and (4) to convey the impact God's culture should have on the world. I hoped that such a project would provide the foundation for Living Word to not only make the necessary adjustments for reaching today's generations but also include a growing structure that could adapt in the years ahead with the goal of reaching all future generations.

My first step was to develop a visitor survey to send both to people who had visited Living Word over the past year as well as to those individuals who have stayed. I hoped that the survey would begin the process of discovering the reasons some people choose not to stay and the reasons why some choose to make our church their home. Below is the survey I developed:

Visitor Survey

This survey is designed to help the leadership understand what is working well and what needs improving. The question allows you to select 6 possible choices from 0 to 5. Please select one of the following for each question: **0 for poor to 5 for good**. Some questions have a choice such as – **Y/N** or other appropriate selections. A **comment** box for each section is provided for any additional thoughts you may wish to express.

Again, thank you for your time!

Circle the number that reflects your thought.

Web:

		Yes	No				
1	If you looked at our webpage, did you find it helpful?						
		0	1	2	3	4	5
	a. Rate the webpage						
		Yes	No				
2	Was the webpage easy to use and user friendly?						
		0	1	2	3	4	5
	a. How easy and user friendly was it?						
		Yes	No				
3	Did the webpage appeal to you?						
4	Did the webpage provide the information you were looking for?						
5	Any further comments or thoughts on our webpage?						

Property and Building:

		0	1	2	3	4	5
1	Did the grounds look neat and kept?						
2	Did the landscaping appear kept?						
3	Was visitor parking available?						
4	Any problems with parking?						
5	Did the exterior of the building look neat and clean?						
6	Any further comments or thoughts on our property and building?						

Facilitating Change to Reach All Generations

Your Experience:

		0	1	2	3	4	5
1	Did someone greet you when you entered the building?						
2	Were you directed to the appropriate ministries and services?						
3	If you had children, were you directed to the age appropriate ministry for them?						
4	If you had children and they were in a particular area of service, did you feel that particular ministry touched your child?						
5	When you entered the main sanctuary, were you greeted again and helped to feel welcomed?						
6	Was the praise and worship uplifting to you?						
7	Any further comments on the praise and worship?						
		0	1	2	3	4	5
8	Did you find the message/teaching relevant for you needs?						
9	Was the presentation of the message/teaching clear and understandable?						
10	Any other comments you would like to make regarding the message/teaching?						

		Too Long	Just About Right	Too short			
11	Was the length of the services good?						
12	Any other comments you would like to make about the overall service?						
		0	1	2	3	4	5
13	If you stopped by the host/hostess counter, how was your experience?						
14	If you stopped by the host/hostess counter, were the people able to help answer any of your questions or concerns?						
15	Your overall experience at Living Word Community Church?						
16	Any other comments you would like to make about your overall experience at Living Word Community Church?						
17	Can you share why or why not you chose to attend Living Word Community Church?						

Once the survey was sent, I began research to gain insight regarding the principles that build strong leadership skills for bridging the generations, especially in light of cultural shifts. This investigation explored the differences between generational concerns and how leaders can effect change by refocusing and prioritizing mission, values, and effective practices for reaching the next generations. Examining issues preventing Living Word from connecting to multiple generations was an important part of my quest. The research provided an important foundation for designing and implementing the ministry intervention.

Once my research was complete, I developed material to train leaders and influencers on the discoveries the research had produced. The goal of this material was to raise awareness regarding the issues and problems Living Word needed to address in order to build a culture that nurtures change, resulting in a system that supports long-term change. This step also focused on developing small-group training materials for current and future leaders on renewing the vision and mission of Living Word Community Church and on developing a structure for implementing the principles for connecting the generations.

After synthesizing my research into a presentation, determining the best approach for communicating the material, and selecting dates to best suit attendees, I built a Facilitator's Guide, Participant's Guide, and a PowerPoint presentation to complement the Participant's Guide. I then designed a means of assessing my endeavors and conducted a training in April 2018—two separate Saturday sessions at Living Word. My goal was to raise awareness of the challenges facing Living Word for reaching the generations and cultivating responsiveness to those challenges through positive changes needed to reach all generations for Christ.

This book represents the research and resources from that project. **Section One** (chapters 2-5) contains the biblical-theological foundation for this book, examining the beginnings of God's cultural project; the responsibility of the cultural project that falls to each generation to communicate its personal values, principles, and experiences to the next generation; the example of Jesus, the maker of culture; and the opportunity that lies in front of believers since Pentecost in going beyond cultural boundaries.

Section Two of this book (chapters 6-8) reviews recent literature on culture, examines the characteristics of the various generations, and presents means of overcoming cultural barriers in order to make important connections between the generations and reach others for Christ.

Introduction

Section Three (chapters 9-13) provides practical resources for use as a study guide, study group notes, reflection questions, sermon notes, or curriculum for other seminar or class instructional settings. It contains a sample seminar agenda and session descriptions as well as a Facilitator's Guide adaptable to your teaching needs.

God's heart is His lost creation, and the New Testament clearly communicates this with the story of Jesus coming, dying, and rising again for all. In a culture that was resistant to Jesus, He exemplified the ability to connect with all generations. With America's culture rapidly shifting, the challenges facing today's churches are only increasing. Christian leaders must discover answers to those challenges and provide solutions for connecting with the generations. The following chapters provide biblical and contemporary research and practical resources to assist in that process.

SECTION ONE

Reaching the generations should be what the church normally accomplishes, but that does not seem to be occurring. Recent research reveals that a shift that has occurred in America's culture that has influenced every facet in society, including the church. American culture is not easy to define due to the plethora of cultures combined together throughout the country. However, a working definition for culture is an aggregate of knowledge, experiences, beliefs, values, attitudes, and behaviors defining and directing a way of life accepted by a group of people.[2]

Another important facet about culture, as Andy Crouch notes, is the idea that culture is what humanity makes of the world.[3] As Scripture is reviewed, this idea emerges from God's intent from creation, from humanity's failures, and from God's intervention into humanity's lostness.

Also, the definition of culture helps clarify that the church has its own culture. This culture of the church—its beliefs, values, attitudes, and behaviors—can sometimes run counter to society's culture. In today's society there are significant challenges facing the church.[4] The greatest counter to today's culture is people learning to function under Christ's lordship of their lives.[5] This is why unchurched people walking into a church may feel uncomfortable, disconnected, or simply not understand what is going on. Unchurched people feel uncertain because the values, beliefs, behaviors, symbols, language, forms, and communication that believers understand often register as foreign to them.

God intended to establish culture so humanity could enjoy life with Him, with each other, and with the world God had created. The next several chapters will explore the cultural project God started at the beginning of creation, examine the alienation and broken fellowship with God due to sin, and then trace God's re-culturing work through the patriarchs, Israel, Jesus, and briefly through the book of Acts.

Chapter 1
The Beginning of God's Cultural Project

The Original Design

From the beginning of creation, the Lord intended humanity to develop and live in culture. He set the foundation, laying the groundwork from the start when He "planted a garden in the east, in Eden; and there he put the man he had formed" (Gen 2:8).6 It was God who established the parameters humanity would live in, the directives for living together, and set the goals for humanity (1:26-28; 2:15-18, 23-25).

As creation unfolds, the biblical story begins revealing a God who is not hidden. Genesis immediately presents the Creator: "In the beginning God" (Gen 1:1). He is the Creator of the world with its uniqueness and beauty, and humanity—the climactic act of His creation. Of all God created, only humans are described in specific detail, emphasizing humanity's importance. To further stress humanity's standing in creation, God spoke to himself to create humans—male and female—in His own image. He did not say for the land or soil to create humankind.7 "Then God said, 'Let us make man in our image, in our likeness...'" (v. 26). Though Adam and Eve were the pinnacle of God's creation, the importance placed on the garden is seen only after Adam is placed there: "The LORD God took the man and put him in the Garden of Eden to work it and take care of it" (2:15). The very words "to work it and take care of it" stress the value of importance God placed on the garden and its contents. This man and woman find themselves, as all humans find themselves, in the midst of an unfolding story.[8]

Insight is provided about this Creator in the first three chapters of Genesis. First, Adam and Eve were created in God's own image. The purpose of this image and likeness was to allow humanity the opportunity for fellowship and a relationship with Him. Humanity was created at God's will and for His pleasure. This is expressed in the book of Revelation; "Thou art worthy, O Lord, to receive glory and honour and power: for thou hast created all things, and for thy pleasure they are and were created"[9] (Rev 4:11, KJV). Second, the humans will be able to commune with this Creator who takes delight in the humans He has created (Gen 1:31; 2:19-20). Finally, humanity will know the pleasure of God's presence, love, and favor through living in fellowship with Him. It was intended for humanity to live dependent on this Creator for life and existence in this world.[10]

One foundational truth for God originating culture emerges in the revelation that the Lord is the first gardener.[11] "Now the LORD God had planted a garden in the east, in Eden; and there he put the man he had formed" (Gen 2:8). Somewhere between the third day of creating plant life and the sixth day, the Lord God planted a beautiful garden specially prepared for Adam.[12] The Lord established a set of values and beliefs as He placed Adam in the garden He planted. Those values and beliefs were set when the Lord fixed boundaries for Adam to enjoy the garden and avoid failure.[13] "You are free to eat from any tree in the garden but you must not eat from the tree of the knowledge of good and evil, for when you eat of it you will surely die" (vv. 16-17). God gave specific but clear directions; Adam and Eve were free to eat from any tree but one, the tree of the knowledge of good and evil. God established value, belief, and boundary, thus creating culture.

As mentioned earlier, culture is what humanity makes of the

world.[14] Crouch shapes this idea about culture—that culture is a choice, it is cumulative, and culture is what people make of their world.[15] It is how humanity makes sense of their world by making something of their world.[16] Three facts substantiate this idea. First, God blessed humanity, instructing them to be fruitful and multiply. Included in this blessing was delegated responsibility for all of the living creatures: "God blessed them and said to them, 'Be fruitful and increase in number; fill the earth and subdue it. Rule over the fish of the sea and the birds of the air and over every living creature that moves on the ground'" (Gen 1:28). Second, when the Lord placed Adam in the garden He planted, God told him "to work it and take care of it" (2:15). Adam's directives were to cultivate, to tend, and to care for this garden.[17] The care and tending to creation is humanity's mission.[18] Third, when Adam and Eve chose to eat from the tree that was forbidden to eat from, they created a different culture that would affect humanity until the end of time (2:16-17; 3:6-8; Rom 5:12-14). Adam was made a responsible being to share in taking care of God's creation; instead he started a counterculture.

A Counterculture Begun

A counterculture started when Adam and Eve failed to keep the culture God established for them. A counterculture runs against the values and beliefs the Lord intended for humanity to live by. Genesis 3 records this terrible event plus the dialogue between Eve and the serpent that led to humanity's downfall.

A glimpse of the cultural values and beliefs Adam and Eve were living by emerges from Eve's encounter with the serpent: "The woman said to the serpent, 'We may eat fruit from the trees in the garden,' but God did say, 'You must not eat fruit from the tree that is in the middle of the garden, and you must not touch it, or you will die'" (Gen 3:2-3). God extended remarkable freedom for humanity when He said that Adam and Eve could eat from any tree in the garden except one. Crouch comments on this freedom: "Culture is the realm of human freedom," containing in this freedom the "constraints and impossibilities," which are "the boundaries within."[19] Boundaries were established in the middle of the garden, in the middle of all of humanity's free choices.

Sin's Corruption of Culture

The serpent's question, "Did God really say, 'You must not eat from any tree in the garden'?" (Gen 3:1) actually denied the love of God and intended to suggest, "How could God keep any good thing from you if He loves you?" The serpent also intended to draw attention away from all the good God had given them and to focus Eve and Adam's attention on the one thing they could not have.[20]

What the serpent did was assist Eve in changing her values and beliefs of the forbidden fruit by raising doubts in the accountability of God's Word, and in His purpose for humankind.[21] Eve's perspective was altered from seeing the fruit detestable and dangerous to the touch to now seeing "that the fruit of the tree was good for food and pleasing to the eye and also desirable for gaining wisdom" (Gen 3:6). The serpent twisted and degraded the divine image that humanity received through craftily and deceitfully describing their personal image of being like God could only be known through a personal experience of knowing good and evil (v. 5).[22] Instead of being a cultivator with God, humanity now is a consumer,[23] as Eve "took some [of the fruit] and ate it. She also gave some to her husband ... and he ate it" (v. 6).

Adam and Eve were not forced to eat what was forbidden; the serpent only helped change their values and beliefs. With craftiness, the devil was able to corrupt the culture God was creating with this one choice Adam and Eve made: "... for when you eat of it you will surely die'" (Gen 2:16-17). Death in the Bible primarily means separation.[24] Through disobedience Adam and Eve broke fellowship with God (3:22-24; Eph 2:12-13; 4:17-18). Since humans are both spiritual and physical beings, following Adam and Eve's disobedience, they died spiritually, and are now at odds with

God. Adam and Eve's rebellion consisted of their rejection of the divine boundaries established by the Lord. Also, Adam and Eve's rebellion was against the good order that God established in His good creation.[25] The immediate effects resulted in humankind experiencing guilt, shame, rejection, weakness, and helplessness.[26] Where humanity would have enjoyed a relationship with God that was built on open communion, love, trust, and security, now Adam and Eve's rebellion produced isolation, defensiveness, blame, and banishment.[27] Instantly, their eyes were opened; now they had knowledge of good and evil but through their own experience. Instead of them being like God, Adam and Eve are now filled with shame, realizing they are naked. The cultural community that God intended for humanity—to experience His presence and to work to cultivate and nurture God's good creation—is now marred with disobedience and rebellion.[28] Humanity now inherits a value system flawed and blemished.[29]

Redirecting Culture's Purpose

The devil was able to warp the culture God had intended, but a new set of values and beliefs would direct the future cultures of this world. Adam and Eve had exchanged their enjoyment of God's fellowship for separation and exile from His Kingdom.[30] Now their nakedness caused them to be aware; they had nothing to hide their guilt.[31] Their very first act after their consumption of the fruit and loss of fellowship with God was to make fig leaves into some type of clothing. Instead of Adam and Eve enjoying the good Garden planted for them with a good God and His presence, they are now trying to protect themselves from broken fellowship with this good God and from one another.[32]

From the sowing of fig leaves onward, culture will be intertwined with sin. From Genesis 3 through 11, culture is spiraling downward as sin ravishes humanity. As humanity increased in numbers, with every new generation, cultures rose and fell. The counterculture that began with a choice in the Garden of Eden is now considered normal, and that culture is ever-changing, increasingly anti-God in its values and beliefs. The culture God intended to establish is considered the counterculture to humanity's progressiveness. Humanity's alienation from God and one another only descends into greater shame, filled with violence and perversion of culture.[33]

Reinstituting God's Culture Project

Originally culture began with God, though that culture was perverted and distorted. Neither God nor His standards or commandments were in any way corrupted, however, God created humanity with a will and freedom to choose. As Henry C. Thiessen notes, "Adam could will to sin or not to sin. After the fall, man's ability to sin became [his] inability not to sin."[34] Adam and Eve only had one bad choice to make in the Garden. Now, humankind is faced with a myriad of good and bad choices every day.[35]

With the whole world fallen, God had a plan to intervene in order to see a culture developed that would be a testimony of His grace. This cultural project was to be established around a set of standards that would direct humanity's decisions for living in a healthy relationship with God and each other.[36] God exemplifies this when He intervenes in Israel's history, choosing and calling a man named Abram (Gen 12:1).

Abram, known better as Abraham, was the father of the Jewish people and eventually the father of all people choosing to live a life of faith in God; as the Apostle Paul writes, "he is the father of all who believe" (Rom 4:11). The importance of Abraham's place in history, especially biblical history, is seen in the fact of his dominance in the Book of Genesis and the shadow he cast extending over the entire Bible.[37]

God singles out Abram for this distinct purpose, to make of him a great nation (Gen 12:2). Just as the Lord God provided a more permanent covering for Adam and Eve, animal skins for fig leaves, God now chooses culture to show His mercy on a vastly grander and longer scale.[38] Through the family of Abram, the Lord God chose to demonstrate to the rest of the world filled with multiple and conflicting cultures how a nation depends on God for its identity, security, and very existence.[39] A believer's hope for growth, meaning, and fulfillment is tied to the understanding of their identity. Understanding who God is and a being's relationship to Him is the foundation of an individual's belief system and his or her behavioral patterns as a Christian.[40]

When the Lord changed Abram's name to Abraham (Gen 17:5), God's agenda was to create something new, something that had not existed before, a nation that belonged to Him in a special way.[41] This cultural project would unfold through Abraham and Sarah's son Isaac, then through Isaac and Rebekah's son, Jacob. This cultural project continued through the twelve children of Jacob and his wives, Leah, Rachel, Bilhah, and Zilpah, and all their descendants. As this project unfolded, Abraham's descendants relocated to a foreign country where their population multiplied, but they eventually found themselves in bondage to the indigenous people of Egypt. The Lord foretold this to Abraham shortly after his call (15:13). Roughly two hundred fifteen years[42] passed before Abraham's descendants moved to Egypt due to a severe famine that plagued the known world (41:56-57). Initially, Pharaoh and the people of Egypt showed hospitality, kindness, and favor to Abraham's descendants. However, as time passed, a new Pharaoh arose, unfamiliar with the reason the Israelites were living in Egypt. This new Pharaoh led his people in fear to act hostilely toward Abraham's descendants. Pharaoh states in Exodus 1,

> "Look," he said to his people, "the Israelites have become much too numerous for us. Come, we must deal shrewdly with them or they will become even more numerous and, if war breaks out, will join our enemies, fight against us and leave the country." So they put slave masters over them to oppress them with forced labor, and they built Pithom and Rameses as store cities for Pharaoh (Exod 1:9-11).

This may not sound like the beginning of a great cultural project, but it sets the stage for God to emerge on the scene as the Redeemer by revealing himself to a man named Moses. Moses's supernatural encounter in Exodus 3 sets the juncture for God to start forming the foundation for His cultural project. Starting a new culture rests more in what God wanted the Israelites to be—that is, seeing with eyes of faith what God was expecting them to become and then striving to embody those values.[43]

God's Cultural Goal

Before moving further into the values of culture, it is important to describe the Lord's goal for this new cultural project. This goal is two-faceted. The first facet is revealed to Moses when he is at the mountain of God (Exod 3:12): "And God said, 'I will be with you. And this will be the sign to you that it is I who have sent you: When you have brought the people out of Egypt, you will worship God on this mountain.'" The first facet is also a sign. This sign includes three parts to it. First, the Lord would be with Moses; second, Moses would succeed in delivering the Israelites from bondage; and third, Moses and the people would worship God at the mountain of God.

The second facet is found in Exodus 19, where a glimpse of God's ultimate purpose for this cultural goal is expressed. The Lord instructs Moses to share with the people:

> Then Moses went up to God, and the LORD called to him from the mountain and said, "This is what you are to say to the house of Jacob and what you are to tell the people of Israel: 'You yourselves have seen what I did to Egypt, and how I carried you on eagles' wings and brought you to myself. Now if you obey me fully and keep my covenant, then out of all nations you will be my treasured possession. Although the whole earth is mine, you will be for me a kingdom of priests and a holy nation.' These are the words you are to speak to the Israelites" (Exod 19:3-6).

This second facet includes four parts. Three of the parts are

The Beginning of God's Cultural Project

directly related to the Lord—either to what He had done or what He would do, if Israel keeps its end of the agreement. First, the Lord stresses that He was the one who delivered the nation of Israel from bondage and brought them to the mountain of God. Though Moses was the point man in dealing with Pharaoh, the Lord makes it clear that He delivered the Israelites from bondage. Second, the condition placed on Israel was that they were to obey God fully and keep His covenant. If they fulfilled the two conditions, then the Lord would keep the two remaining parts of this second facet. The third part, God would make the nation of Israel His own treasured possession, and fourth, a new identity will be provided; they are to become a kingdom of priests and collectively grow into a holy nation.

With regard to the Lord stating that Israel was to become a kingdom of priest and a holy nation, this idea is found in the New Testament as well: "But you are a chosen people, a royal priesthood, a holy nation, a people belonging to God, that you may declare the praises of him who called you out of darkness into his wonderful light" (1 Pet 2:9). The idea is also found in John's Revelation. John was banished on the Island of Patmos as a prisoner for faithfully preaching the Word of God and sharing about Jesus. While John lived banished there, he received the final word or vision from the Lord recorded in the book of Revelation.[44] As John initially encounters Jesus, he receives this revelation of Jesus Christ and writes, "To him who loves us and has freed us from our sins by his blood, and has made us to be a kingdom and priests to serve his God and Father—to him be glory and power for ever and ever! Amen" (Rev 1:5-6).

The cultural goal of the Lord for Israel is the same for the Church. It involves freedom from slavery of sin; it also entails learning to worship God in a way that pleases Him and discovering the joy of being a treasured possession, a holy nation, and a royal priesthood.

Facilitating Change to Reach All Generations

Values of the Cultural Project

This cultural project begins with God; He is the foundation stone or the "chief cornerstone" (Matt. 21:24). Just as at creation when God established the values of the culture He set up for humanity, He will again create the values for this new cultural project.

As the book of Exodus begins, centuries have passed, and now God is calling Moses, for He has heard and seen Israel's hardships. Moses had served in the court of Pharaoh, but now Moses is serving as a shepherd, tending the flock of his father-in-law in the land of Midian[45] (Exod 2:15). It is important to point out that Moses was not seeking or looking for the Lord, but the Lord sought Moses out (3:1). In Exodus 3, the Lord God uses a supernatural manifestation to attract Moses—a burning bush that is not consumed. When Moses turns to look at this strange phenomenon, the Lord speaks to him. As Moses draws close, the Lord calls from the midst of the flame to him. God knew Moses's location and his name; He knew the exact moment that Moses would pass that spot of the burning bush, and He knew the desperate plight of the Israelites.

> The LORD said, "I have indeed seen the misery of my people in Egypt. I have heard them crying out because of their slave drivers, and I am concerned about their suffering. So I have come down to rescue them from the hand of the Egyptians and to bring them up out of that land into a good and spacious land, a land flowing with milk and honey—the home of the Canaanites, Hittites, Amorites, Perizzites, Hivites and Jebusites. And now the cry of the Israelites has reached me, and I have seen the way the Egyptians are oppressing them" (vv. 7-9).

The above verses provide revelation of the attributes and decrees of God in His calling Moses.[46] He sees, hears, and is concerned about the harsh suffering of the people of Israel. In Exodus 2 God expresses His concern: "God heard their groaning and he remembered his covenant with Abraham, with Isaac, and with Jacob" (2:24). The next verse says, "God looked on the Israelites" and was concerned (v. 25). Also, the Lord God used this burning bush experience to reveal something about His own character and glory to Moses. God reveals "the glory of His unchanging, mediated salvation which remains the hope and encouragement of those who are in slavery and bondage."[47]

As Moses turns to investigate this strange manifestation, immediately God identifies one of His moral attributes, holiness.[48] The Lord begins to teach Moses about His holiness by not allowing him to proceed too far.[49] The Lord told Moses that the ground he was stepping onto was holy, so Moses must remove his sandals. The ground did not become holy due to Moses stepping onto that sacred soil; God's presence made it holy (Exod 3:1-5).[50] Once his shoes are removed, Moses stops proceeding closer, and hiding his face, he hears God identify himself, "I am the God of your father, the God of Abraham, the God of Isaac and the God of Jacob" (v. 6). The reference of the patriarchs shows Moses that this is not a new or unknown God, but One who made a covenant with the fathers of the nation Israel and remembers His promise to them.[51] God's covenant-relation to His people is humanity's best support and greatest encouragement to faith.[52]

Though this story includes Moses's call and commissioning, it really is about God's concern and compassion for the Israelites and the covenant He made with Abraham. "I will make you into a great nation and ... all peoples on earth will be blessed through you" (Gen 12:2-3). Once again, just as the Lord God had created culture in the Garden of Eden, He is about to start this cultural project with slaves, a culture that was to be defined by faith.[53] Robert Lewis and Wayne Cordeiro affirm that a church looking to create culture must begin with God's purpose and anchor their values in His kingdom.[54]

Interestingly, the Lord announced He would come down to rescue the Israelites from their misery and distress; however, Moses is assigned the responsibility to accomplish that task (Exod 3:9-10). The Lord had chosen Moses, an eighty-year-old fugitive running from Egyptian justice, to accomplish the impossible task "of leading 2.5 million crushed and hopeless slaves out of the control of the mightiest empire on earth."[55] Moses's response to the mission the Lord was calling him to was to declare his insecurity of feeling like he was a nobody: "Who am I?" (v. 11) he asked. The Lord met Moses's insecurities and sense of inadequacy with the promise of His presence and the assurance of success (v. 12). The Lord felt that the full and complete adequacy of His presence was enough to meet any challenge Moses would face.[56] The theme of God's presence is one of the major subjects in Exodus.[57]

Core Values for the Cultural Project

One of the core values for this cultural project is **God's abiding presence.** The importance of this is stressed when Israel sins by worshipping the golden calf (Exod 32:7-8). God removes His presence and promises an alternative (33:2-3). The value of the presence of God was so important to the culture that Moses asked the Lord not to move the nation of Israel without promising to go with them (v. 15). Moses knew the impossibility of trying to govern the people and support them in the desert; he wanted to lead the people in confidence and assurance, knowing that God's presence would indeed go with them.[58]

God's presence was the unique characteristic of this cultural project. However, the people had forfeited God's favorable presence through their disobedience of worshipping the golden calf.[59] Moses understood the importance of this loss, for it was the mark that was to distinguish the people of God from those who were not God's people (Exod 33:12-16). The people of God are to be presence driven more than program or purpose driven; "those who are led by the Spirit of God are sons of God" (Rom 8:14; Gal 5:16). Also, this is an important core value for this cultural project, a presence driven culture.[60]

Another uniqueness of God's presence as a core value is the fact that though it was essential for the community, it is also vital for the individual. Returning to the unfolding dialogue between Moses and the Lord, the Lord responds to Moses's objection to go to Egypt with the promise of His abiding presence and guidance,[61] which should have been enough for Moses.[62] God's promise contains two elements: first was God's assurance that He would go with Moses and provide direction. Second, God promises success and the sign of success:[63] "When you have brought the people out of Egypt, you will worship God on this mountain" (Exod 3:12). God's purpose for this deliverance was so the children of Israel could worship Him at the mountain of God. This is stressed frequently in the book of Exodus (4:23; 7:16; 8:1, 20; 9:1, 13; 10:3, 7-8, 11, 24, 26; 12:31).[64] The Hebrew word "worship" is the same word for "serve" or "to be a slave."[65] The Israelites were serving as slaves to the Egyptians, but after the Lord delivered them and brought the Israelites to the mountain of God, they would serve and worship Him as His subjects.[66]

Another value important for this cultural project is **God's name.** Moses questions the Lord on what name he is to provide the elders of Israel if they were to ask for it. The Lord God provides, "I AM WHO I AM" (Exod 3:14). In the past, those who knew the Lord before Moses's encounter on the mountain of God knew God as El or Elohim, or as El-Elyon—that is, the Most High. They also knew Him as Shaddai—that is, God the Almighty. Yet, the name the Lord gives to Moses is Yahweh. This name was known as far back as the time of Seth; however, it had been lost over time. Yahweh is the name God chose, for it is His only personal name; all the rest are titles.[67] This revelation is renewed with God officially calling to Moses and giving His personal name.

Also connected with this value of God's name is His calling Moses by *his* name. From the burning bush and by addressing Moses personally through this pattern of speech, "Moses! Moses!", God was using a form called "repetition of endearment. In ancient Semitic culture, addressing someone by saying his or her name twice was a way of expressing endearment, that is, affection and friendship."[68] This is amplified not only by the fact of the Lord expressing His endearment and friendship to Moses by calling his name twice, but also by the Lord giving Moses His personal name, *Yahweh.*

One final value to be woven into the very fabric of this new culture is the **importance of the blood of the lamb.** Even with all the judgments God passed on Pharaoh and Egypt, Pharaoh never gave up his opposition to the will and purpose of Jehovah until the lamb was slain.[69] The Passover was the final plague that would cause Pharaoh to submit to God and release the Israelites from their bondage (Exod 11:1; 12:12-13).

The importance of the blood in God's cultural project goes back to the gates of Eden.[70] God took the skin of animals to provide a better covering for Adam and Eve (Gen 3:21). The skin covering was more than just better clothing than the fig leaves Adam and Eve made for themselves. It refers to God's willingness to provide for Adam and Eve's shame and acceptance of them. This step to cover Adam and Eve was also a foreshadowing that animal sacrifices would benefit humanity and the sacrifice of Jesus's blood on the Cross.[71] From the gates of Eden to the final close of Scripture, it is the blood that unites the beginning and the end, restoring what sin had destroyed.[72]

Cultural Principles

One of the principles of this cultural project is that **it would unfold over time,** bearing a complex but rich testimony to the world the Lord God loves. An important principle regarding culture is that it is not created instantly but takes time to build, develop, and shift as it reflects and responds to God's interventions.[73] God's agenda was to create something that had not yet existed: a nation, a group of people who belonged to Him in a special way. As Creator of heaven and earth, He wanted to be represented to the nations as One dwelling in the midst of Israel.[74]

Obedience is another principle associated with God's desire for Israel to become His treasured possession and a kingdom of priests (Exod 19:5-6). It also was a condition God placed on Israel, that they would have to fully obey and keep the covenant God would make with them. This principle of obedience God expected was more than some sort of national treaty between himself and Israel. The contract God instituted at Sinai involved each Israelite believer, and He expected each one to commit to it. The Lord considered this "commitment as binding as the vows taken by bride and groom at a wedding ceremony. Their very hearts and wills were called for, not just a pledge of allegiance on the part of the group."[75] The Lord expected and required each person in the nation of Israel to be completely faithful and obedient to the covenant He was about to reveal.[76]

One unique aspect relative to this principle of obedience occurs during Israel's first encounter at the mountain of God: that He expects full obedience from the entire nation. Moses receives instructions from God, and then Moses gathers the elders of the tribes of Israel, setting "before them all the words the Lord had commanded him to speak" (Exod 19:7). The people respond in unison, "We will do everything the Lord has said" (v. 8). All of this is happening before the Lord has given the first commandment, the first instruction on worship, or any other demand on the people. In other words, from these words Israel "pledged themselves to make obedience to God the guiding principle of their life."[77] By faith, the people of Israel said, "yes" to whatever God would lay down for them to obey. It was after this commitment from Israel that the Lord stated He would descend on Mount Sinai in a dark cloud with thunder and lightning.

Another principle initially presented to Moses during his calling is **God's holiness** (Exod 19:12-13, 21-22). In Exodus 19, this principle of holiness is being extended to Israel, and its importance is stressed when God instructs Moses to tell the Israelites a second time not to touch the mountain: "The LORD said to him, 'Go down and warn the people so they do not force their way through to see the LORD and many of them perish'" (v. 21). An interesting point emerges on God's holiness. When Moses receives his calling, he turns to look at the bush. As he steps toward the bush, God warns Moses not to come any closer and to remove his sandals, for the ground is holy. Moses stands on that holy ground, and the Lord instructs Moses to have the people prepare themselves for God's manifestation on the mountain. The people are to wash their clothes and abstain from sexual activity to be ready on the third day for God's presence to descend on the mountain (vv. 10-12).

After the people consecrate themselves and on the third day, Moses takes the people out of the camp to the mountain so they can meet with God. At the base of the mountain, Moses and the people wait as the whole mountain becomes engulfed with smoke as the Lord descends in fire. The whole mountain trembles violently, and the Israelites hear the sound of a trumpet, which grows louder and louder. Then Moses calls to the Lord and He responds. The people of Israel literally hear God speak to Moses, calling him to come up the mountain (Exod 19:9, 14-20). When Moses proceeds up the mountain, God warns Moses to instruct the people not to approach the mountain, emphasizing again His parameters of holiness. God is setting the stage for Him to speak the Ten Commandments to the people.

In Exodus 20, the very first verse "emphasizes that God spoke the Ten Words/Ten Commandments himself directly to Israel rather than through the intermediation of Moses."[78] The preamble and prologue appear in verse 2, identifying the parties involved in this covenant agreement: "I am the Lord your God who brought you out..." (Exod 20:2). In the preamble, Israel is the recipient, identified by the "you," and the "Lord God" identifies himself as the giver of the covenant. The latter part of verse 2 is the prologue, explaining how the parties came to be related. It states, "who brought you out of Egypt, out of the land of slavery" (v. 2). Since the Lord had rescued Israel from slavery, He has a claim to the people.[79]

The Beginning of God's Cultural Project

With Moses and the people at the base of the mountain, God speaks the Ten Commandments audibly to them. The Ten Commandments would become the principles guiding this new cultural project.

Another principle revealed in Exodus 20 is **the fear of the Lord** (v. 20). Hearing God speak audibly, along with seeing Mount Sinai consumed in smoke, hearing the thunder and seeing the lightning, and hearing a trumpet blowing, the Israelites tremble in fear. The Israelites experience sensory overload in this remarkable manifestation of God, and they misinterpret this whole experience. The Israelites determine that they only want Moses to speak to them, for they conclude they would die if God continued to speak to them (vv. 18-19). The people's decision is a choice of convenience.[80]

Moses makes it clear that this powerful demonstration from the Lord has a specific purpose; God is testing them because He wants them to fear Him, but He does not want them to be afraid of Him (Exod 20:20). Instead of being in awe of God, the people shrink back in intimidation, retreating from God's presence. A further explanation of God's manifestation is that Moses reassures the people that God's closeness is a means of testing them to see if they really will be afraid of sinning and disobeying Him.[81]

Worship is another principle for the new cultural project. There are several keys to this principle. First, specific instructions on worship are communicated to the people (Exod 20:22-25). The Israelites are not to make any image to be brought alongside the Lord God as an equivalent or rival with Him.[82] Second, the Lord provides the Israelites a brief overview for constructing altars in anticipation of their need to worship Him now that He is their covenant God.[83] A third key for corporate worship that the Lord expects of the Israelites is separation from the foreign people of the Promised Land (23:24). This key also includes a warning. God warns the Israelites not to allow any of the foreign people to stay in the land. The reason for this emphasis is that the foreign people would corrupt the Israelites, leading them to worship false gods (vv. 32-33). A fourth key for this principle is service. Included in the

Israelites' worship is service (3:12): "And God said, 'I will be with you. And this will be the sign to you that it is I who have sent you: When you have brought the people out of Egypt, you will worship God on this mountain.'" The NKJV and the ESV changes the word "worship" for "serve" in the later part of that verse: "you will serve God on this mountain." Worship and service are connected, and the point is that God expects both from His people.

God's cultural project is taking shape with values and principles set. The Israelites see that God is committed, and He expects them to be as well. The Lord God expects the Israelites to demonstrate their commitment through obedience to His commandments, through expressions of worship and service. However, success of this project will also rest on the Israelites passing on what they learned and experienced to all future generations. Though several items deserve consideration associated with the cultural project, it is imperative to move ahead in this cultural project. With the cultural principles established, attention turns to the transition of leadership.

Chapter 2
A Cultural Responsibility

The responsibility of the cultural project rests on every present generation to communicate these personal values, principles, and experiences to the next generation. This requires more than just passing on the rules and demands of the legal aspects of this cultural project. It demands the communication of the personal and powerful experience of God's presence, His love, grace, and mercy. Moses makes it known in Deuteronomy 7 that God's choice of Israel was marked by grace:[84]

> The LORD did not set his affection on you and choose you because you were more numerous than other peoples, for you were the fewest of all peoples. But it was because the LORD loved you and kept the oath he swore to your forefathers that he brought you out with a mighty hand and redeemed you from the land of slavery, from the power of Pharaoh king of Egypt. Know therefore that the LORD your God is God; he is the faithful God, keeping his covenant of love to a thousand generations of those who love him and keep his commands (Deut 7:7-9).

The biblical concept of grace includes these ideas of being gracious—showing favor and lovingkindness. Thus, Moses's statements in Deuteronomy, "The Lord ... set his affection on you ... [and chose] you ... because the Lord loved you" are all references of God's grace. The fact that God entered into a covenant with the Israelites was an act of His grace. This is further emphasized when God gave the self-revelation to Moses on the mountain after the Israelites had sinned with the golden calf (Exod 34:6-7).[85] In these verses God is declaring to Moses His characteristics:

> And he passed in front of Moses, proclaiming, "The LORD, the LORD, the compassionate and gracious God, slow to anger, abounding in love and faithfulness, maintaining love to thousands, and forgiving wickedness, rebellion and sin."

Another statement made by the Lord God during Moses's call in Exodus 3 needs reviewing as well. The reason for reconsidering this statement in Exodus 3 is that it is foundational to this entire cultural project. Though highlighted earlier in this review, it was not stressed until now. It is important to understand that although this statement was spoken in the past, it still relates to the present:

> God also said to Moses, 'Say to the Israelites, The LORD, the God of your fathers—the God of Abraham, the God of Isaac and the God of Jacob—has sent me to you. This is my name forever, the name by which I am to be remembered from generation to generation' (Exod 3:15).

Of course, verse 15 follows verse 14 where the Lord provided the name Moses would tell the elders. God shared His personal name, "I AM WHO I AM" (v. 14). *Yahweh* is the name God chose for the Israelites to know Him. *Yahweh* was His personal Name; all the rest of the names used for God are titles.[86] This personal name of God was to be passed on from generation to generation. From *God's Word Translation*, the latter part of verse 15 states, "This is my name forever. This is my title throughout every generation" (Exod 3:15, GW).[87] Just as Moses received instruction to pass on *Yahweh's* personal name to the next generation, so does every generation carry the responsibility to communicate the personal name of the Lord to the next.

Cultural Mentoring

It is not made exactly clear why or when Moses chose Joshua as his aid, but Joshua is introduced when the Israelites are traveling from Egypt to the mountain of God. Though it is not stated until later in Israel's journey, Joshua is more than Moses's aide, he is Israel's future leader (Deut 1:38). The following events are part of Joshua's training as the future leader.

It is interesting that Moses chose Joshua in preference to other leaders older than forty years of age. Presumably, Moses had found him to possess unusual gifts of courage and godliness, which is why when the Amalekites attacked the Israelites, Moses tells Joshua,[88] "Choose some of our men and go out to fight the Amalekites" (Exod 17:9). It could be said that this is Joshua's first step in his training to become the next leader under Moses's supervision and support. Here is the point: Moses saw certain qualities that encouraged him to choose Joshua.

God tells Moses to record the victory over the Amalekites on a scroll and be sure Joshua hears it. From the *New Living Translation*, verse 14 states, "Write this down on a scroll as a permanent reminder, and read it aloud to Joshua" (Exod 17:14, NLT2). Moses is building this future leader by reminding Joshua that God used him to defeat the Amalekites. In addition to recording this victory and reciting it to Joshua, Moses builds an altar and worships the Lord, for Moses is being sure the Lord receives credit for the victory. A new name of the Lord is introduced in this moment of worship, *Jehovah-nissi* (Exod 17:15, KJV) or *Yahweh-nissi*, which means, "the LORD is my banner" (Exod 17:15, NLT). Under His banner, in His name and strength, believers win the battles they face.[89]

Joshua was included as Moses's aide when Moses, Aaron, and his sons, along with the seventy elders, were invited to ascend to a place on the mountain where they would see God. Moses was providing Joshua with the opportunity to experience these once in a lifetime encounters with the Lord God. This group of men see God on His throne with a pavement of sapphire under His feet, and as these leaders approach, God does not raise His hand against them (Exod 24:11). In addition, these men drink and eat a meal before God. Apparently, food and drink were prepared by heaven for these leaders. The NLT states, "In fact, they ate a covenant meal, eating and drinking in his presence!" (v. 11). *The Bible Knowledge Commentary* affirms this idea that the leaders, including Joshua, were ratifying the covenant with a meal.[90]

Though Joshua is not mentioned in the invitation earlier, he must have been in the midst of all of this activity, for it is here that he is identified as Moses's aid (Exod 24:13). Joshua is the only one out of the seventy elders and Aaron and his sons to receive this invitation to accompany Moses further up the mountain of God. Moses instructs the elders to wait for him and his assistant, Joshua, for they would return to them (Exod 24:14). There is no record that the Lord told Moses to bring his assistant with him, but there is also no record that the Lord objected to Joshua accompanying Moses.

However, Moses leads this younger person to accompany him to experience God's unique presence. Moses and Joshua travel up the mountain to a specific location, and the glory of the Lord covers the mountain. With Joshua at his side, Moses waits for six days in the glory until the Lord specifically calls for Moses only to proceed further (Exod 24:15-16). This experience must have left an indelible mark on Joshua's soul, for a few chapters later when Moses attends to the Tent of the Lord, the text states, "The LORD would speak to Moses face to face, as a man speaks with his friend. Then Moses would return to the camp, but his young aide, Joshua, son of Nun, did not leave the tent" (33:11).

A Cultural Leader

At the fringe of the Promised Land, the Israelites are ready to enter the land. A decision is made to send twelve spies, one from each tribe, to explore the land (Num 13:1). Ten spies report negatively about the land; the rest of the Israelites start to grumble and complain against Moses and Aaron (14:2). Joshua and Caleb, the only two from the twelve spies who gave a positive report, join Moses and Aaron in trying to convince the people of Israel not to rebel against the Lord (vv. 5-9). However, the people fail to learn the needed lessons of faith and trust. Fear spreads faster than faith. In despair, the congregation blames Moses, Aaron, and God for a defeat that had not yet occurred.[91] Joshua, on the other hand, as a man of faith, reaffirms the appraisal of the goodness of the land as he declares his complete trust in the Lord's ability to defeat Israel's enemies and deliver the land and its people into their hands.[92]

When the time comes for Moses to hand over the responsibility of leading the Israelites over to Joshua, Moses encourages Joshua with these words: "You have seen with your own eyes all that the LORD your God has done to these two kings. The LORD will do the same to all the kingdoms over there where you are going. Do not be afraid of them; the LORD your God himself will fight for you" (Deut 3:21-22). As Moses prepares to transition the nation of Israel from his leadership to Joshua's, he recites a previous victory to remind and encourage Joshua in what God has done and what He has promised.[93] Moses is obeying God's command to encourage Joshua; "Your assistant, Joshua son of Nun, will enter it. Encourage him, because he will lead Israel to inherit it" (1:38).

Cultural Failure

Unfortunately, Joshua does not follow the same pattern of mentoring someone to follow in his footsteps. When Joshua reaches the end of his life, he has not finished the task of fully taking possession of the Promised Land. Now the cultural project is left to future generations unfamiliar with God's great acts of the past. This idea is expressed in the following verse: "Israel served the LORD throughout the lifetime of Joshua and of the elders who outlived him and who had experienced everything the LORD had done for Israel" (Josh 24:31). Regrettably, Joshua's lasting epitaph is found in this statement: Israel served the Lord no further than the elders who had served with Joshua.[94] Once the elders all passed, "another generation grew up, who knew neither the LORD nor what he had done for Israel" (Judg 2:10).

With all of Israel's failures, including their rebellion and God's judgment, "the prophets are convinced that God has not abandoned His plan" for this cultural project.[95] The Old Testament is laced with prophetic hope. From Genesis to Malachi, *Yahweh* provides hope that One who could help all of humanity was coming. When recounting the travels of Israel, Moses declares:

> The LORD your God will raise up for you a prophet like me from among your own brothers. You must listen to him. For this is what you asked of the LORD your God at Horeb on the day of the assembly when you said, "Let us not hear the voice of the LORD our God nor see this great fire anymore, or we will die." The LORD said to me: "What they say is good. I will raise up for them a prophet like you from among their brothers; I will put my words in his mouth, and he will tell them everything I command him" (Deut 18:15-18).

Isaiah also foresees a day when all the nations will gather at the mountain of God:

> In the last days the mountain of the LORD's temple will be established as chief among the mountains; it will be raised above the hills, and all nations will stream to it. Many peoples will come and say, "Come, let us go up to the mountain of the LORD, to the house of the God of Jacob. He will teach us his ways, so that we may walk in his paths." The law will go out from Zion, the word of the LORD from Jerusalem (Isa 2:2-3).

> Here is my servant, whom I uphold, my chosen one in whom I delight; I will put my Spirit on him and he will bring justice to the nations. He will not shout or cry out, or raise his voice in the streets. A bruised reed he will not break, and a smoldering wick he will not snuff out. In faithfulness he will bring forth justice; he will not falter or be discouraged till he establishes justice on earth. In his law the islands will put their hope (Isa 42:1-4).

Though Israel had not completely fulfilled their role in God's cultural project, God had promised prophetically of One who would—Jesus. Not only would Jesus fulfill God's expectations of God's cultural project, but He also would be the ultimate cultural cultivator. Jesus is the turning point in history, fulfilling God's original purposes spokes to Abraham: "all peoples on earth will be blessed through you" (Gen 12:3).

Chapter 3
Jesus, Culture Maker

Introduction

Luke records the coming of John the Baptist, the forerunner of the coming Messiah (Luke 1:13-17). Once John emerged into the public eye, he clarified his purpose. "As is written in the book of the words of Isaiah the prophet: 'A voice of one calling in the desert, Prepare the way for the Lord, make straight paths for him'" (3:4). John prepared the peoples' hearts for Jesus.

Out of the four biographers of Jesus's life, two include genealogies, which are critically important. The reason the biographies are important is that they point to Jesus's humanity and that He has a cultural inheritance. Matthew traces Jesus's lineage back to Abraham, which is significant. "Genealogies assert that the story being told is not simply a timeless myth, it is anchored in a particular group of people in a particular place."[96] Matthew boldly and abruptly declares, "A record of the genealogy of Jesus Christ the son of David, the son of Abraham" (Matt 1:1). Matthew highlights Jesus's continuity with David, the king of messianic promise and Israel's royal house, and links Jesus with Abraham, the father and founding ancestor.[97]

Luke postpones his genealogy until he has told about Jesus's miraculous conception, His birth, the spiritual activity at His dedication (Luke 2:25-38), and His childhood.[98] Then Luke begins Jesus's genealogy with this striking statement: "He was the son, so it was thought, of Joseph, the son of Heli" (3:23). This may seem like a strange way to begin a genealogy, but Luke had already taken the time to tell of Jesus's miraculous conception in great detail. Luke is making it clear that Joseph is not Jesus's biological father.[99] Luke's genealogy accomplishes two things. First, it clearly leads the reader to the conclusion that Jesus is "the son of God" (v. 38). Second, it makes the case that Jesus is fully and completely human. He is the son of David, the son of Abraham, the son of Adam, and the Son of God (vv. 31, 34, 38). Luke is stressing that Jesus is completely human and that He has a cultural inheritance. This is also the reason Luke goes into great detail to stress Jesus's genealogy, to emphasize the concern with the continuity of culture that exists with Jesus. If Jesus was not a cultural being, then He was not human at all. However, Jesus followed customs and traditions.[100] Luke makes this clear when he writes, "When he was twelve years old, they went up to the Feast, according to the custom" (2:42), and "He went to Nazareth, where he had been brought up, and on the Sabbath day he went into the synagogue, as was his custom. And he stood up to read" (4:16).

Culture Cultivator

Jesus did not just pass on Israel's culture inheritance, though the early years of His life were spent learning and living the culture of His people. Jesus was not just absorbing and practicing culture in order to innovate ways to bring himself into conflict with the nation's leaders. Scripture provides little of Jesus's years of development—only a couple of glimpses reveal He was discovering His identity and purpose. When Jesus was twelve years old, and His parents accidentally left Jerusalem without Him, they looked for Him for three days before finding Him in the temple. When Jesus was corrected by His earthly parents, He was surprised that Mary and Joseph did not understand that He would not be in His Heavenly Father's house (Luke 2:49). Following this brief revelation of the twelve-year-old Jesus, Luke goes on to say, "And Jesus grew in wisdom and stature, and in favor with God and men" (v. 52). The important idea here is, though Jesus understood His identity as being the Son of God, He still lived out His divinity in a normal life as a young Jewish adult in Nazareth subject to His earthly parents. It is amazing to consider that the One who created all of heaven and earth lived out His early life as an ordinary person, not concealing His divinity.[101]

When the time had fully come, Jesus emerged onto the scene to initiate His public ministry (Mark 1:14-15). Jesus did not merely come to pass on His cultural inheritance but to bring something new to the world. The Gospel of Mark provides a synopsis of the new; the good news of God, the kingdom of God being near, and repentance and faith were all some of the new Jesus was bringing. "Jesus went into Galilee, proclaiming the good news of God. 'The time has come,' he said. 'The kingdom of God is near. Repent and believe the good news!'" (vv. 14-15). The Greek word for "time" is *karios*, meaning a specific or distinct point in time. The implication is that Jesus knew it was the right time to initiate the plan of salvation.[102] As stated already, culture is an aggregate of knowledge, experiences, beliefs, values, attitudes, and behaviors defining and directing a way of life accepted by a group of people. Though Jesus was a Jew, raised in the Jewish culture, it was not the Jewish culture that He was looking to propagate. The culture Jesus would begin to communicate was that the kingdom of God was near. In other words, Mark was stating that the kingdom of God was near in the person of Jesus. However, foundational to this new culture is the behavior— repentance and faith—required for entering this Kingdom.

A major part of Jesus's message was, "the kingdom of God is near" (Mark 1:15). This is emphasized when Jesus sends His disciples out to preach and heal the sick. The disciples are told to tell the people that "the kingdom of God is near" (Luke 10:9, 11). This is one of the values of this new culture, "seek first his kingdom and his righteousness" (Matt 6:33). Jesus did not mean an earthly kingdom but a spiritual one that was present, referring to God's rule, reign, dominion, and sovereignty in the hearts of people.

Another value in this kingdom culture is God having rule over a person's heart, and Mark points this out, highlighting the fact that the reign and rule of God had started to take place in the life and ministry of Jesus Christ. As a result of this present but spiritual kingdom, Mark highlights a distinctive element in Jesus's message to the people; they must believe the gospel.[103] This new culture would be one of faith, believing was crucial.

Herein lies the key: "The people were amazed at his teaching, because he taught them as one who had authority, not as the teachers of the law" (Mark 1:22). The gap between the rabbis and Jesus did not lie in the subject matter being taught but in His own person. Jesus knew fully that He was the Son.[104]

The Gospel of Matthew presents Jesus teaching a radically new way of thinking. The Sermon on the Mount provides the basic principles for living in the kingdom of God or the expected behavior of this new culture. It is not the wise and talented who share or take possession of the kingdom of God or heaven but the "poor in spirit" (Matt 5:3). The God's Word (GW) translation puts the verse this way: "Blessed are those who recognize they are spiritually helpless. The kingdom of heaven belongs to them" (v. 3, GW). Jesus is not referring to the physically poor, those so impoverished that they may revert to begging to survive.[105] The culture Jesus is creating begins with an improvised spirit, with an understanding that those trying to enter the kingdom are spiritually helpless.

Jesus's teaching was creative as He established new standards for living in this Kingdom culture. How foreign and culturally challenging were Jesus's teachings as He continued with the Sermon on the Mount: "Blessed are you when people insult you, persecute you and falsely say all kinds of evil against you because of me. Rejoice and be glad, because great is your reward in heaven, for in the same way they persecuted the prophets who were before you" (Matt. 5:11-12).

Jesus was not just providing some new information when He spoke of the kingdom of God; it was near. However, the good news He shared included a comprehensive restructuring of the social life that people would live.[106] This restructuring tackled the deeper issues the Law could not address. In the Sermon on the Mount, Jesus moved the Law's external focus to the internal state of the human heart. Jesus's "prescription for changing the heart involves changes in culture."[107] The following excerpts from the Sermon on the Mount highlight this focus on behavior changes that address the heart:

- Matthew 5:20, "For I tell you that unless your righteousness surpasses that of the Pharisees and the teachers of the law, you will certainly not enter the kingdom of heaven."

- Matthew 5:22, "But I tell you that anyone who is angry with his brother will be subject to judgment. Again, anyone who says to his brother, 'Raca,' is answerable to the Sanhedrin. But anyone who says, 'You fool!' will be in danger of the fire of hell."

- Matthew 5:23-24, "Therefore, if you are offering your gift at the altar and there remember that your brother has something against you, leave your gift there in front of the altar. First go and be reconciled to your brother; then come and offer your gift."

- Matthew 5:28, "But I tell you that anyone who looks at a woman lustfully has already committed adultery with her in his heart."

- Matthew 5:38-39, "You have heard that it was said, 'Eye for eye, and tooth for tooth.' But I tell you, Do not resist an evil person. If someone strikes you on the right cheek, turn to him the other also."

- Matthew 5:43-45, "You have heard that it was said, 'Love your neighbor and hate your enemy.' But I tell you: Love your enemies and pray for those who persecute you, that you may be sons of your Father in heaven."

Jesus set new standards that were to dictate the kind of behavior His followers were to demonstrate to their neighbors and enemies. This new social lifestyle would demonstrate what it looks like to live trusting and depending on God. The greatest innovation Jesus offered was not the alternative culture He proposed but the life He lived out in front of everyone. Coming full circle, what Israel could not accomplish in their original calling, to demonstrate complete dependence on *Yahweh*, Jesus fulfilled. He fully lived a life totally and completely dependent on *Yahweh*. He did not compromise even when faced with the Cross. Jesus literally turned the other cheek, allowing the Roman soldiers to fully abuse and brutally destroy His body. But for the brokenness of culture to be dealt with, Jesus had to accept the calling of the Cross.[108]

Jesus's creative cultivation of culture also included reshaping the Passover meal. He reinterpreted the cup and bread to reflect His death.[109] The bread speaks that the Bread of life was broken in death in order that life could be given to those who were spiritually hungry and in need. The cup states that Jesus poured out His blood, which is His life, in order that life could be received for life, is in the blood (Lev 17:11). That blood cleanses a person and includes a quickening power.[110]

The Cross and Culture

Long before Jesus was ever crucified, the cross already existed. Many had died on a cross before Jesus; however, no other human being before or since Jesus's death on the Cross adequately accomplished what He did. Jesus suffered the full weight of humanity's sin and rebellion against God. Scripture states, "God made him who had no sin to be sin for us" (2 Cor 5:21). Jesus's death on the Cross for humanity provides the complete deliverance from the burden and curse of sin.[111] "Christ redeemed us from the curse of the law by becoming a curse for us" (Gal 3:13). "The strangest and most wonderful paradox of the biblical story is that its most consequential moment is not an action but a passion, not a doing but a suffering."[112] The Cross was not only the symbol describing how Jesus died, but Jesus made it clear that all who would follow Him would need to deny themselves and take up their Cross (Matt 16:24; John 10:18; 1 John 3:16).

Though the Cross extinguishes all life, creativity, and cultivation[113] according to human understanding, it really sets the platform for the kind of culture the Church needs to exhibit. That is, the culture the Church should display is one of self-sacrifice, laying down one's life for others, serving others, being motivated by love, and living a life accentuated with the Spirit's presence and power (Luke 24:49; John 13:13-15, 34-35; Acts 1:8; 2:1-4; 1 John 3:16). Conceptually, this new culture Jesus introduces is fleshed out in the epistles. The book of Romans strongly emphasizes the point: "Don't you know that all of us who were baptized into Christ Jesus were baptized into his death? ... In the same way, count yourselves dead to sin but alive to God in Christ Jesus" (Rom 6:3, 11). In Galatians, Paul highlights this extremely well: "I have been crucified with Christ and I no longer live, but Christ lives in me. The life I live in the body, I live by faith in the Son of God, who loved me and gave himself for me" (Gal 2:20). In several of his epistles, Paul makes it clear that a person following Christ is to be dead.[114] In Colossians, Paul says, "For you have died, and your life is hidden with Christ in God" (Col 3:2, ESV). The Church was to be characterized by this self-sacrificing love, demonstrated through serving one another and the communities the Church found itself in.

The Resurrection and Culture

As impacting as the Cross is for cultivating culture, it was the Resurrection that was a culture-shaping event. The Resurrection is the most culturally significant event in all of history, having changed more cultures and more people than any other event in history.[115] So powerful was this event that it transformed the disciples from a group of individuals afraid they might be crucified next into a fearless band who would give their lives without hesitation (John 20:19; Acts 4:13).

The Resurrection was so powerful that believers in the first century began to hold their church services on the first day of the week. Understand that the Sabbath was written into the Ten Commandments as well as into the story of creation. For the Jewish believers to begin to make this shift was a significant cultural move. This is found in Acts, "On the first day of the week we came together to break bread. Paul spoke to the people…" (Acts 20:7; 1 Cor 16:2). This is the first clear indication that the first-century believers were beginning to make Sunday, the first day of the week, a time for gathering together and worshipping. However, it is clear that the first-century believers still would congregate on the Sabbath. Paul and Barnabas met with people on the Sabbath (Acts 13:42, 44). Though Paul and Barnabas met with people on the Sabbath, they also met with people on Sunday for worship, prayer, and fellowship.[116]

The crucifixion and resurrection of Jesus Christ is the culmination of God's culture-rescuing project that began in Genesis 12. Jesus faced the worst that humanity had to throw at Him only to triumph overall, even humankind's sinfulness and rebellion. More than just a spiritual triumph, it was also a cultural victory. Jesus's victory over death, hell, and the grave is the pronouncement that the arrival of God's realm of possibility—His Kingdom—is made manifest in humanity's cultural structures. Jesus's victory is also the good news that the kingdom of God is available to all peoples of the world.[117] "In the kingdom of God, a new kind of life and a new kind of culture becomes possible, not by abandoning the old but by transforming it. Even the Cross, the worst that culture can do, is transformed into a sign of the kingdom of God, the realm of forgiveness, mercy, love, and indestructible life."[118] The Cross set the platform for the Book of Acts and the story of culture to move throughout the known world, transforming lives and impacting culture.

Chapter 4
Beyond Pentecost and Cultural Boundaries

Acts is about culture[119] and the transformation of lives. From the three thousand people who received salvation on the Day of Pentecost, to countless individuals responding to the gospel of the Kingdom, to entire towns and regions impacted with this good news, all are evidence of the gospel's power to impact lives and culture (Acts 2:41; 8:5-8; 13:44, 49).

The story that unfolds in Acts is one about cities. The story begins in Jerusalem and ends in Rome. In between these two bookends are stops along the way, touching just about every commercial and political center around the Mediterranean Sea. Almost all of the activity of the gospel moving through the Roman Empire took place in urban centers.

One of the themes in Acts is that God is on the move, and He is no longer telling the story in just one culture. The call for salvation is to every person and every cultural group: "Everyone who calls on the name of the Lord will be saved" (Acts 2:21). However, the group at the beginning of Acts on the Day of Pentecost is entirely Jewish (having made pilgrimage to Jerusalem for *Shavuot*) and is still identified with the cultural project of Israel (v. 5).[120] A shift begins with Peter going to Cornelius's house in Acts 10. The moment Peter walks across the threshold of Cornelius's house, the mission of Jesus extends beyond the cultural specificity of Israel.[121] Not only was Cornelius's whole house saved and transformed, but they were also filled with the Holy Spirit (10:44-46). Even the religious people had to acknowledge that God had extended repentance unto life to the Gentiles as well (11:16).

The ministry that began in Acts 2 entirely directed to the Jewish people shifts again in Acts 17 where Paul is speaking to Greeks. Paul tries to relate to the Greeks by preaching a message closer to Peter's sermon in Acts 2, which receives a response, "'What is this babbler trying to say?" (Acts 17:18). Others remark, "He seems to be advocating foreign gods" (v. 18). Luke then comments, "They said this because Paul was preaching the good news about Jesus and the resurrection" (v. 18).

Initially, Paul's message was foolish to the Greeks, but when Paul met again in the Areopagus, he changed his approach and adjusted the message. Before meeting these philosophers, Paul had walked through Athens and noticed that the city was full of idols. In the process of touring Athens, Paul found an idol to an unknown god. Paul connected this group of Greeks by using that idol and began to tell them about God (Acts 17:22-23). Then Paul defined the Creator God of the Bible; He is the One who created the world and everything in it (v. 24).[122] Paul wisely led his hearers from the beginning of creation to their need to seek this God who sustains everything and everybody, to the resurrection of Jesus from the dead (vv. 25-31).

A statement Paul makes conveys the importance and necessity of learning to communicate the Good News to all generations: "In the past God overlooked such ignorance, but now he commands all people everywhere to repent" (Acts 17:30). This follows another important statement made by Barnabas and Paul on their first missionary trip: "In past generations He allowed all the nations to go their own way" (Acts 14:16, HCSB). However, God did not give up on His plan of redemption or His purpose of blessing all the nations of the earth through fruitful seasons of harvest.[123]

When Paul and Barnabas return from their first missionary travel, they share with their community of faith in Antioch all that the Lord had accomplished through them. Again, this dynamic team shares a remarkable phrase that makes it known that God has provided all of humanity the opportunity for salvation. Paul and Barnabas's testimony was that "God had ... opened the door of faith to the Gentiles" (Acts 14:27). The Greek emphasizes that "a door" of faith was opened to the Gentiles, meaning it was a specific door for the rest of humanity.[124] Now God's cultural project is extended to all peoples in all cultures of the world.

Conclusion to Section One

From the beginning, God intended a culture that would demonstrate a populace dependent on Him, a race of people living in a trusted relationship with Him. However, humanity chose a different path and produced a counterculture to God's plan. Just as humanity changed their values and beliefs, this generation has shifted in values and beliefs. Instead of humans being cultivators with God, they are now consumers.[125]

A gap exists between the Christianized world and the non-Christian or the secular world.[126] America once fostered a culture that was friendly and receptive toward the gospel message but now is drastically turning away from the gospel though still spiritually hungry. Reaching the generations involves more than just learning their characteristics and how and what they believe. True, differences do exist between the generations, but each group was not born in a vacuum. The culture of America has shifted, and it is clear that many churches today do not consider or really understand that shift. The culture of America intentionally works to inoculate generations against the teaching of the Bible, believing the Bible offers no answers and is antiquated. Society now faces a crisis, and the church does not fully understand what is happening.[127]

In spite of humanity going counter to God's culture, God had a plan, and He prophetically spoke of a future help that rested in the coming of His Son, Jesus Christ. In the meantime, while the Lord God waited for "the fullness of time" (Gal 4:4, ESV) to come, He chose a people to begin a cultural project, hoping to demonstrate what it would look like to live in a trusted relationship with God, based on grace and faith. Through this cultural project, God intended that the nation of Israel would exemplify to the world a culture of faith and trust as they lived the principles of life.

Instead, Israel as a nation failed in this project except for a faithful remnant (Rom 11:29, 31). However, a plan was already in place for rescuing the project. Jesus not only demonstrated what it looked like to fully obey and trust God the Father, He established the culture the Church should live in this lost world. Jesus's life, death, and resurrection provide the opportunity for every human to experience the life God intended as they cultivated a culture supporting that life.

The culture God intends today is one filled with people whose lives are transformed. It is a culture that honors God's presence and reveres His holiness. It is counter to the present, postmodern, secular, humanistic culture of America. However, it also is a culture that welcomes all peoples without judgment or criticism. I designed the following diagram to illustrate the culture shift from modern to postmodern:

To reach all the generations, the church needs to understand the negative effect the postmodern, secular, humanistic culture is having on every facet of society; this includes the church. Yet believers need to focus not on the negative impact that secular culture has on the church but on how powerful a presence-driven culture can transform lives. The church needs to nurture a culture and atmosphere that communicates the genuine and authentic presence of God. The goal the church needs to strive for is one that allows the distinguishing presence of God to manifest while providing opportunity for all generations to experience that presence for themselves.

SECTION TWO

This section explores the potential barriers preventing the church from effectively connecting with and drawing younger generations into its congregation. The complexity of the issue requires much more than simple changes in method or practice. John Drane makes a statement that captures the essence of the challenge that church leaders face: "unchurched people would typically have no sense at all that the Church might enrich their own or their children's lives."[128] This statement puts the challenge into perspective, revealing that the issue is bigger than understanding the characteristics and preferences of different generations.

Cultural and ideological shifts have changed people's view of the church entirely,[129] and a significant number of people are wondering why so many Christians are mean-spirited.[130] This is supported through research presented by David Kinnaman and Gabe Lyons in their book, *unChristian*. Kinnaman and Lyons found that outsiders, people who were not in the church, viewed modern-day Christianity as no longer being Christian.[131] To Kinnaman's and Lyons's surprise, their research uncovered a growing hostility toward Christians. Outsiders perceive clearly what Christians stand against, even sensing that Christians are angry, violent, and illogical.[132]

While the Church does affirm that change has occurred in society, many believers do not understand how far culture has shifted. The America many of the congregants grew up in, a modern society still influenced by the church, is now a postmodern and a strongly secular humanistic society.[133]

In addition to this change in culture, there exist two categories of people. The first category contains the different generations co-existing, and the second category is what Drane describes as seven distinct groups of people that the church will need to relate to if it is to fulfill its missional mandate.[134] Most local churches today deal with three different categories of Christians: cultural Christians, congregational Christians, and convictional Christians.[135] The increase in technology usage poses yet another challenge for churches. People of all ages can now readily access information anywhere and anytime. In the midst of sermons, congregants can Google to verify the factual nature of any statement made. To complicate this further, people's access to the world of information allows them to know what is happening on the other side of the world in moments and sometimes as an event actually is happening.[136]

President George W. Bush summed up the events after September 11, 2001 when he stated that a "new normal" existed for the world in which we live.[137] That phrase, "new normal" describes the change that has occurred in our culture and world. The church has not really caught on or figured out how to respond to this change, but it is going to have to figure out how to live in this "new normal," learning to navigate such challenges.[138]

While it may be tempting to point a finger to blame the media or some other force for luring the younger generation away from church involvement, this sort of blaming does not bring about desired outcomes. As American culture has changed, the Church itself has reacted in many ways that have not welcomed the younger generation. Local churches must assume partial responsibility for the fact that the younger generation does not want to attend or connect. Some church members' actions have likely unintentionally hurt the church's relationship with young newcomers. On one particular occasion a person in the church chastised a visiting young man who wore his hat into the sanctuary. This visiting young man was an unchurched person who took his hat off but after that service never returned. In other words, the concern was more about the hat than the lost soul of a person. That church should have represented Jesus better than that.

Section Two

In *unChristian*, Kinnaman and Lyons explore six areas about which people outside the church, including the younger generations, have negative images and perceptions of Christians within the church. Though a couple of these perceptions have always been around, the American culture has birthed new ones that churches have to learn to navigate in this age of skepticism.[139]

In my search to discover why our church was failing to connect well with the younger generations, a warning emerged. *Relevance* is a term used often to describe the efforts churches make to connect with those who view traditional churches as irrelevant or out of touch. It is important to be relevant but not at the expense of allowing the biblical Jesus to be hijacked. One cannot justify separating what are perceived as the negative aspects of the Christian faith and just portraying Jesus as a big-hearted, open-minded, moral teacher who never offends. Jesus taught some tough truths about humanity and sin.[140] The challenge for churches is to present the Jesus of the Bible who was loving, merciful, and compassionate but who also strongly denounced sinful behavior.

Today, a church that is intergenerational is really a counter-culture itself. The church's culture is one that segregates and isolates, all in the name of ministry. We have children's church, varied aged focused student ministries, young adult ministries, and then the church is expecting all generations to interact with each other in worship.[141] Yet, ministry needs to develop that is consistent with the Bible, reflecting all generations worshiping together.

The following chapters first offer a brief description of the postmodern, secular, humanistic culture in which Americans now live. Next, they briefly describe the different generations, provide some distinguishing characteristics of the seven distinct groups Drane identifies, and examine the three distinct groups of people within the church. (A plethora of material exists on these topics, but for our purposes, a brief overview will suffice.) The chapters then present six negative perceptions that outsiders, including the younger generations, have of the church; they cover twelve *sticking points* that could help the generations connect (i.e., "stick together") or that could actually become points of conflict; and finally, they provide an understanding of the leaders' roles in reaching the next generation, leading change, and leading an intergenerational ministry.

Chapter 5
Understanding Culture

The culture of the United States of America is primarily Western or European in origin and form, though it is influenced by the multicultural ethos of the many distinguishing ethnic groups within America. The American culture includes the customs and traditions of the United States, which means it also "encompasses religion, food, what we wear, how we wear it, our language, marriage, music, what we believe is right or wrong, how we sit at the table, how we greet visitors, how we behave with loved ones, and a million other things."[142] Diane Chandler states that culture "influences implicit and explicit social norms, patterns, and expectations in the framing of values, which in turn affect how [people] think, feel and relate to and care for others."[143] It is important to understand that the way people live and interact with each other is all related to culture.

America combines a plethora of cultures, making understanding "American" culture somewhat difficult. Also, the word *culture* has become the new buzzword in mainstream media, which uses it with a slightly different purpose of promoting an agenda of acceptance and tolerance. This only confuses the meaning of *culture*, not only in our society but within the church as well. The following list from

Facilitating Change to Reach All Generations

Texas A&M University affirms the difficulty of defining culture. The list is divided into groups for easier comprehension but to also emphasize the struggle of placing a simple label on culture:

> Culture refers to the cumulative deposit of knowledge, experience, beliefs, values, attitudes, meanings, hierarchies, religion, notions of time, roles, spatial relations, concepts of the universe, and material objects and possessions acquired by a group of people in the course of generations through individual and group striving. It is the systems of knowledge shared by a relatively large group of people. Culture is communication, communication is culture.[144]

The complexity of trying to define culture is only exasperated with the inclusion of behavior and the way people do life together:

> Culture ... is cultivated behavior; that is the totality of a person's learned, accumulated experience, which is socially transmitted, or more briefly, behavior through social learning. A culture is a way of life of a group of people—the behaviors, beliefs, values, and symbols that they accept, generally without thinking about them, and that are passed along by communication and imitation.[145]

And if the prior info on culture is not enough, symbols and patterns are thrown into the mix convoluting the definition more:

> Culture is symbolic communication. Some of its symbols include a group's skills, knowledge, attitudes, values, and motives. The meanings of the symbols are learned and deliberately perpetuated in a society through its institutions. Culture consists of patterns, explicit and implicit, of and for behavior acquired and transmitted by symbols, constituting the distinctive achievement of human groups, including their embodiments in artifacts; the essential core of culture consists of traditional ideas and especially their attached values; culture systems may, on the one hand, be considered as products of action, on the other hand, as conditioning influences upon further action.[146]

Finally, the last two statements from Texas A&M University wrap up this detailed definition of culture:

Culture is the sum total of the learned behavior of a group of people that is generally considered to be the tradition of that people and that is transmitted from generation to generation. Culture is a collective programming of the mind that distinguishes the members of one group or category of people from another.[147]

From this list of descriptive characteristics defining culture, it should be clear that culture influences everything. Culture even affects the way information is transmitted, the use of time and space, and how authority is viewed.[148] From this list a working definition of culture is as follows: an aggregate of knowledge, experiences, beliefs, values, attitudes, and behaviors defining and directing a way of life accepted by a group of people. This list also helps to define the church's culture. The church has its own culture that often runs counter to society's culture. This explains why some unchurched young people who walk into a church may feel lost. The church has its own set of values, beliefs, behaviors, symbols, language, forms, and communication that often registers as foreign to the unchurched.

Another aspect that is important for understanding the challenge facing the church is what Soong-Chan Rah calls, A Tale of Two Cultures. They are the primary and secondary cultural systems that have two different focuses. Rah defines the primary culture as being tribal and personal, one that makes people a priority, and one in which survival depends on relationships. Rah classifies the secondary culture as industrial and impersonal, where the priority is objects, and one in which survival depends on knowledge. Both of these cultures operate by distinct value systems and have different impacts on society.[149]

The Prevailing Culture

Not only has the world influenced America's culture; America's culture has also influenced the world. With regard to size, "America is the third largest country in the world,"[150] and yet, considering the diversity of culture it is one of the most diverse.

Despite this plethora of cultures existing in America, a prevailing culture influences the country as a whole. Americans live in an increasingly secular and postmodern[151] culture with a growing number of people in communities knowing little of the traditional church. This lack of knowledge and misunderstanding of the church has in no way prevented people from having a spiritual hunger.[152] The values and attitudes of modernity have been rejected, but that does not mean they have been replaced with another worldview.[153] Even though countless resources focus on the distinct characteristics of specific age groups and generations, those distinct characteristics are not so self-contained[154] with their particular grouping or generation. As an example, many writers reference the millennial mindset, which generally refers to people born from 1981 to 2000. The traits of this millennial way of thinking commonly appear among people identified as Boomers and Gen Xers. Granted, the younger generations do live with a millennial way of thinking; however, the issue is more than just a generational issue; it is also cultural. Millennials were not born in a vacuum or with their particular beliefs and values; something or someone is producing and forming the worldview and values of Millennials and Gen Zs.

Though postmoderns do not place their philosophy into a defined box, the following characteristics appear to be elemental:

- "There is no absolute truth."[155] Postmoderns look at truth as a contrived illusion, misused to gain power over others.

- "Truth and error are synonymous. ... What is fact today can be error tomorrow."[156] Facts are too limiting to determine anything.

- "Self-conceptualization and rationalization"[157] replace traditional logic and objectivity. Postmoderns reject the scientific method of determining facts and rely on opinions.

- "Traditional authority is false and corrupt."[158] Postmoderns speak against the constraints that religion places on morals and secular authority. They conduct an intellectual revolution against traditional establishment.

- The fair way to administer goods and services is through collective ownership. Modernism has produced disillusionment. Postmoderns feel remorse and regret over the unfulfilled promises of religion, science, technology, and government.

- "Morality is personal."[159] Postmoderns consider ethics to be relative and morality left to personal opinion. This leaves postmoderns free from feeling they have to follow traditional values and rules, allowing each person to establish their own code of ethics.

- "Globalization supersedes nationalism. ... National boundaries are a hindrance to human communications,"[160] and nationalism leads to war.

- "All religions are valid."[161] Postmoderns value inclusiveness of all faiths, denouncing the Bible's exclusive claim that the only way to God is through Jesus Christ, and they gravitate toward New Age religion.

- For postmoderns, liberal ethics should triumph; they support the homosexual and feminist causes.[162] A majority of postmoderns approve of same-sex marriage.[163] Postmoderns declare that they offer a choice, or freedom, which stands in opposition to what the moderns offer, and that is fate.[164]

Pro-environmentalism dictates behavior in a postmodern mindset, and Western society is to blame for the destruction of "Mother Earth."[165]

Basically, the postmodern philosophy is largely a reaction against the values, beliefs, philosophical assumptions, and the constructs of Enlightenment that modernity held. The postmodern denies this Enlightenment and espouses faith in technology and science as instruments of human progress and yet, postmoderns blame the development of technologies for the killing that occurred during the World Wars on such a massive scale.[166] What is also surprising is that postmodernity is not something that emerged with the Millennials. In the *Challenge of Postmodernism*, postmodernity is traced back to 1939 when Arnold Toynbee used the term "postmodern" to suggest that the modern age ended in 1914. What emerged from the ruins of the World War I should be described as "Post-Modern."[167] American culture continues to be saturated with this philosophical idea, propagated at different levels of society. Every corner of the country bears the mark of postmodernity's influence. Ross Parsley calls this the cultural tidal wave.[168]

The Challenge

Reaching younger generations requires more than just learning specific characteristics of a certain age group or learning what should or should not be said or done. Such tactics fail to address the "cultural revolution" that is transpiring. The church's response to this unfolding revolution has been to posture itself to protect beliefs and programs.[169] Many churches have been battening down the hatches against this cultural change, but now those "other people" (the Millennials, and Gen Zs) are moving into communities, challenging the status quo, and disrupting the norm of church life.[170] Some churches are opting to survive and just focus on trying to keep the saints as happy as possible.[171]

The culture that many American Boomers, Traditionalists, Gen Xers, and some very early Millennials grew up in was strongly influenced by the church and identified as Judeo-Christian; now, it is identified as being secular humanistic and postmodern.[172] In today's culture, the church finds itself competing with activities that pull people from church. This cultural change is affecting the church's culture.

The contemporary church also finds itself dealing within three different categories of Christians. The first group is called cultural Christians. This group believes they are Christians because the culture they lived in told them they were. In other words, it is their heritage. The next group are called congregational Christians. The individuals who make up this group are similar to the cultural Christians, except congregational Christians have some connection to congregational life. The final group, convictional Christians, are individuals who actually strive to live their faith.[173] The experience of being a believer is real to this group, and their heart's desire is to live under the Lordship of Jesus Christ.

Another challenge has emerged. Just a little over forty years ago, the church knew only its own community, town, or part of the city. Now, people in the church know what happens on the other side of the world immediately.[174] This availability of information not only changes culture, it changes the church's culture and the people who attend.

Many Christians know changes have occurred but attribute that change to individuals who are completely indifferent to the gospel and the church. However, that does not mean that all Gen Xers, Millennials, and Gen Zs are opposed to the church. Yes, some remain indifferent, and some pose increasing opposition to the church in America. That does not mean that the indifference of the younger generations is related to their being closed to the gospel or the church.

To summarize, postmodernism is difficult to clearly define because the postmodern premise is that no definite terms, boundaries, or absolute truths exist. Part of the reason for this is that postmodernists vary in their beliefs and feelings on matters of concern. The varying beliefs and opinions are due to their presupposition that Western society is corrupt. This view of the Western world's corruption motivates some postmodern individuals to break free from traditional authority. Postmoderns push for freedom from authority centers on their belief that the West's system is inept, that the West relies heavily on traditional values based on irrelevant customs. They also believe that the West's stance on capitalism and nationalism no longer apply in today's culture. They see the West as consumers of natural resources with an outdated lifestyle that hurts the environment.[175]

These challenges that the church faces should not cause believers to retreat but to rise up and seek the Lord for answers about reaching the generations. The book of Acts reveals that the church spread from Jerusalem to Rome under one of the most difficult cultures in history. Jesus instructs the Church that though He was "sending [us] out like sheep among wolves. [We are to] be as shrewd as snakes and as innocent as doves" (Matt 10:16).

Chapter 6
Understanding the Generations

Understanding culture provides insight into the generations. Just as culture has shaped the generations, so the generations have been shaping culture. Major decisions made by one generation have shaped culture while also affecting the next generation. In his book, *Sticking Points*, Haydn Shaw states, "you cannot understand the ... generations without understanding [the] Traditionalists because they built the organizations we have today and trained the Baby Boomers."[176] Gary McIntosh supports this idea by clarifying the Builder Generation comprised of the G.I.s, the Silents, and War Babies, who Shaw calls Traditionalists, all developed a similar perspective on life that strongly influenced Boomers.[177]

If one is going to understand other generations, then this concept of generations shaping culture is key. No matter what generation a person is a part of, each feels at home in his or her own generation. With that said, that does not mean one cannot visit other cultures, learning to appreciate them while learning their language.[178] In other words, if one wants to connect, then one needs to identify the distinctive cultures that other generations live by, such as their values, beliefs, ways of communication, and worldview.

Different Approaches

Dealing with the different generations has its challenges. Shaw presents four distinct approaches to the four generations.[179] Three of these responses are negative, and the fourth approach is the most appropriate and effective.

The first response is to *just ignore them.* As the next younger generation came of age and emerged on the work scene, it was possibly easier for the older generation to ignore what they did not understand. However, as the Millennial population increases and the younger generation fills more positions in society, it will be harder to ignore them.[180]

The second response is to *try to fix them.* It does not work to try to train the younger generations to conform to the principles the previous generation has established and found effective. The thought behind this method is that if the younger generations can just learn to be more like the older generation, then everyone will get along, fulfilling the church's vision and mission. The problem is that the younger generations are not broken, and those of us who are older spend too much unproductive time trying to fix them when the younger generations do not think there is anything wrong.[181]

The third response is to *attempt to make a deal.* If the younger generation cannot be ignored, nor fixed, then perhaps they can be convinced to compromise. In other words, the older generation can bend their guiding principles a bit in order to create a win. As an example, when Gen Xers entered the work force, they did not see why a dress code was needed. After a decade of business leaders ignoring, stereotyping them, and trying to fix them, a deal was made with the Gen Xers; casual Friday is now a standard in many organizations.

The church has fought (and in some cases still fights) over clothing such as suits, ties, jeans, sneakers, flip-flops, shorts, hats, and other dress items. The result has been that the younger generation has just stopped coming or moved on to other congregations or organizations that do not mind what they wear.[182]

This last approach is really more relational. The previous three approaches deal with managing, but this last approach is focused on leadership. "Leaders love their people,"[183] so they do not ignore them nor try to fix them or make deals that really do not accomplish the purpose of vision and mission. Leadership begins by **understanding the people and understanding the differences between the generations.** The Boomer generation was the last to respond to a management style of leading. The younger generations generally respond to relational leadership.184

The Generations

Though there are six generations living in America, the five prominent ones are the Traditionalists, Boomers, Generation X, and Generation Y or Millennials, with the Generation Z or Boomlets just beginning to emerge. Most of the following material comes from Shaw's book, *Sticking Points*, providing a brief look at the characteristics of the five generations.

The Traditionalists

The Traditionalists, born before 1945, are also called the Builders, and include the G.I. Generation, the Mature/Silents, and the War Babies.[185] One cannot understand other generations without first understanding the Traditionalists, for they built the organizations in existence today and trained the Boomer generation. The youngest Traditionalists are still living and, in the workplace, exerting tremendous influence on the organizations they built, which in turn is influencing culture.[186] The Great Depression and World Wars I and II shaped this generation. Traditionalists learned to sacrifice and show patience. They had saved the world, and then they came home and built a nation.[187]

Traditionalists had "more confidence" in ... "leaders" and "large organizations" because they witnessed how the "large hierarchical organization could get things done."[188] They in turn built strong hierarchical organizations using what they learned, a command-and-control approach. Employees were expected to fall in line, do their duty, and prove their loyalty.[189]

This generation was made up of doers who were assertive, loyal, had a strong work ethic, were excellent team players, and kept their jobs for life. They saw marriage as a lifelong commitment, viewed having children out of wedlock as unacceptable, and were avid readers.[190] There was a rapid migration from the farm to the city with this generation. Post-World War II saw multiple subdivisions spring up on the periphery of most major cities in America.[191]

Baby Boomers

Baby Boomers, born between 1946 and 1964, were trained and educated by the Traditionalists during the time America was growing, building, and prospering. It was the best of times, marked by hope, opportunity, and the feeling things would get better.[192] "Boomers grew up as the most optimistic generation"[193] in the history of America. Communities were not ready for the explosion of growth that occurred across the country. Hospitals did not have enough beds; schools were not prepared for the number of students enrolling, and "colleges and universities did not have enough faculty or living space."[194] This overcrowding and lack of space created an atmosphere of competition, teaching Boomers that to get what you want, you have to compete. This meant that everyone may make the Little League team, but only the best got to play.[195]

The Boomers grew up in "the most economically optimistic times"[196] in American history; they changed the "value system from sacrifice to self."[197] Affluence explains the Boomers' distinctive values; "affluence funded the focus on self and the optimism that made the Boomers' growing-up years magical."[198] Boomers grew up being told they were special; thus the "me" generation was born.[199]

Boomers were the first generation to have the influence of TV. In 1963 when John F. Kennedy was assassinated, it was said that it "was the first time the nation cried together."[200] Television brought the images of Kennedy's assassination to every corner of the country.[201]

The move from the farm to the suburbs created a subculture—the teenager. Before the Second World War, the word "teenager"[202] was seldom used, because teens were considered just a younger version of adults. After World War II, marketers saw the profit of this younger generation uninterested in buying their parents' fashions and focused on appealing to this emerging generation.[203]

Along with this newly rising subculture emerged a generation gap. With the Traditionalists' ability to provide the American dream, they could not believe the drop in educational achievement and the rise in drug use, teen pregnancies, and crime. Home was competing with the influences of teachers and the media. The Traditionalists could not believe that their values were undercut by the educational system, creating a gap with their kids.[204]

Boomers were the first generation who considered divorce acceptable and began being tolerant of homosexuality.[205] There are three significant shifts in values among Boomers. The first was in reference to moral values—"sex, authority, religion, and obligation to others."[206] The second shift was in social values—"money, work, family, and marriage."[207] The third was with respect to self-fulfillment. Also, "Boomers were the first generation to have the money, time, and freedom to explore self and search for meaning."[208]

The oldest and youngest Boomers had different experiences and opportunities. Older Boomers had more in common with Traditionalists, came of age with the optimism and idealism of the Kennedy years, and reveled in the success of the space program.[209] The younger Boomers had more in common with Generation X. This group of Boomers grew up with Watergate and the Arab oil embargo, and they lacked the same optimism as their older predecessors.[210] To attract aging Boomers today, new words or terms are needed. As an example, the word "senior," refering to the elderly, is not an accepted term by most Boomers. To the Boomer over fifty, senior means someone they are not—old, elderly, and having reached the golden years.[211]

Generation X

The next group is called Generation X, born between 1965 and 1980. The metaphor Shaw used to describe this generation is *Donkey Kong,* the video game. "The game 'symbolizes the unrelenting challenges' this generation had to overcome. Just as Donkey Kong had to swing through the jungle to overcome different tests and trials, hoping to land on his feet without falling to his death, the Gen X'ers had learn to roll with the bad news and shifting cultural challenges, hoping to land firmly on their feet to survive."[212] Many of the Gen Xers were called the "latch-key kids," due the fact that many wore a key around their necks so they could let themselves into an empty house or apartment after school. Though they were isolated, this Generation was street smart.[213] They also often had to deal with divorce or career-driven parents.[214]

Gen Xers faced multiple recessions, global competition, and the rising tide of missing children whose pictures ended up on milk cartons. Gen Xers became realists as they coped with life's never-ending challenges, learned to roll with the bad news, and realized they did not want to dedicate themselves to the game of life like Boomers. The result was that Boomers misunderstood the Gen Xers, saw them as cynical whiners and called them slackers in the workplace.[215] However, Gen Xers were not whiners but "open-eyed realists" who saw the world differently than Boomers.[216] From the Gen Xers' perspective, it did not make sense to them to keep the same "high expectation as if the world had not changed."[217] Not only had the world changed, it was continuing to evolve, moving from the moorings of the Traditionalists and Boomers. The Gen Xers were not slackers; they were just rewriting the game or world they inherited, and they were beginning to do it with new technology and with new expectations. "Get real" was the phrase the Gen Xers embraced to challenge the older generations to stop trying to spin that everything would be OK, that it would have a happy ending.[218]

Gen Xers are not trying to save the entire world; their focus is on rescuing and protecting their neighborhood. Even though they can be entrepreneurial, they are still individualistic. Gen Xers do not value government in the same way their parents did, nor do they really see the importance of big business. They were raised in a time when society was transitioning from the analog world to the digital world. Many remember starting school without computers, but before graduating high school, computers were being introduced as tools for learning. Gen Xers are eager to make their relationships work, and they want to be there for their kids. They want to have a chance to contribute, to learn, and explore, but Gen Xers tend to be committed to self rather than a specific career or an organization. One looming cloud for Gen Xers was the rise and spread of AIDS.[219] This was the first fatal disease in history that did not require any quarantine, and it had no cure

Gen Xers are skeptical. Due to the economy going bust, the Gen Xers lost confidence in the American dream. Many Gen "Xers began their adult life with unprecedented personal debt"[220] from college as expenses quadrupled and grants and other aids were slashed. Though they were pessimistic and suspicious, three out of four Gen Xers were ambitious and wanted to succeed. They were the first generation to question the story behind the story on their computers and to feel that the news would always be shaded by someone's perspective. In other words, Gen Xers believed that you could not believe everything you were told.[221]

Generation Y/Millenniums/Millennials

Generation Y, also called Millenniums or Millennials, were born between 1981 and 2000. They are also known as "The 9/11 Generation,"[222] the second Baby Boom, or the Echo Boom, and this baby boom of growth was larger than the original Baby Boomers.[223] Some have classified this new generation America's next great generation.[224]

Millennials have an attitude that treats others the way they get treated. They will ignore those who ignore them.[225] They also "expect to be taken seriously, even though they do not have any 'real-world' experience."[226] Millennials do not necessarily believe what they are being told right away, nor do they believe a person's sincerity because they look at leaders and others as not being real.[227] After nine months on a job, Millennials get bored and then act like it is their Gen Xer manager's problem—and, Shaw states, "it is" their problem. The reason Gen Xers and Boomers are responsible is, Gen Xers and Boomers are the ones who taught Millennials to think this way.[228] Millennials need more recognition and praise and want to be doing meaningful work, not just working.[229]

The difference between the parents of Millennials and Boomers is that Millennial parents hovered over their children nurturing them. The president of Wake Forest University called these parents "helicopter parents" due to their constant involvement and oversight. Parents actually became more like activities directors as they arranged and managed play dates, soccer games, ballet, swim team, music lessons, and anything else their Millennial children wanted to do. When Millennials grew to college age, their parents were just part of the package.[230] In general, Millennials value higher education, for they understand that a good career is dependent on having a college degree.[231]

A huge contrast exists between Boomers and Millennials. Millennials saw their parents as an assist, and they would seek advice from them regularly. Boomers did not see their parents as a resource, nor did they feel they needed their parents. Boomers saw their parents as part of the system and part of the establishment. Millennials on the other hand saw their parents as a resource for everyday life issues; they sought their parents for advice, and for help, especially when it came to work. It would not be unusual for employers to have Millennial parents tag along with their children for a job interview.[232] Shaw provided this advice for employers if the parents walked in for the interview with their children: "engage them."[233]

Millennials are different in their self-esteem; many are confident and encouraged to express their feelings, and their parents worked to shield their self-esteem. Thus began the generation of no losers, they were told repeatedly that they were special, and everyone received a trophy for participation.[234] They are the first generation to not know what it is not to have a computer, a phone, the Internet, and Google at their fingertips. They were raised as consumers. The world to a Millennial is a 24/7 place in which one can get just about anything desired, access everyone's information, and connect socially with anyone through the Internet. Millennials do not live to work but prefer an environment that is relaxed, complete with open communication, support, and accolades.[235] They are less loyal to their jobs than previous generations.[236]

Millennials are the "most racially and ethnically diverse [generation] ... in American history."[237] By the year 2000, one-third of the total population of the Millennials were nonwhites and Latinos. That is almost 50 percent more than the Boomer generation and nearly 200 percent higher than those born before 1946.[238]

Generation Z/Boomlets

The current generation is known as Generation Z or the Boomlets. Those born after 2001 fall into this category. Generation Z will change the behavior and culture of America because 49% of those born into this generation were Hispanic. In 2006, the number of

Gen Z births outnumbered the start of the Baby Boomers. They will easily grow to be the largest generation and the most technologically advanced group in the history of America. This technological advancement is due to the fact that most have flat screen TVs, computers, and livestreaming capabilities in their rooms. Video games are a standard with most Gen Z as well as smart phones. This group does not know what it means not to have computers or smart phones in their world. With computers and web-based learning, this generation is trading their toys for electronic ones at a much younger age. Gen Zs are more aware of the advantages of the web and computers; therefore, they are savvy consumers, knowing what they want and how to get it. This generation is oversaturated with information from every angle: Internet, web TV, Netflix, Amazon, Google, and a variety of social media options.[239]

Another Challenge

Drane describes seven distinct "groups of people as a cultural and missional analysis."[240] He looks beyond the generations and points out that the Church will need to relate to these seven distinct groups if it is to fulfill its missional mandate.[241] The seven distinct groups or categories do not exhaust all that exist within our culture, nor is there a strict demarcation between each group.[242] This kind of information provides awareness that our culture is more openly diverse than the Church is generally willing to accept. In addition, this information exposes the overall centrality in which the church ministers, meaning, churches are reaching people just like themselves or just certain kinds of people. The traditional values of the church are not embraced by the culture, nor are the traditional methodologies of churches reaching the people. "A more useful way of understanding people in relation to the mission of the church will be to try and identify how they are dealing with the rationalization and apparent meaninglessness of life."[243] That last statement focuses more on the cultural and missiological analysis for understanding the different groups of people the church needs to reach.

Below is a brief definition of each group that the church will need to relate to if it seeks to fulfill the Great Commission mandate.

The Desperate Poor – One of the rapid changes that has occurred within our culture is the dramatic increase in the number of people living in poverty. The gap is widening between those who have and those who have not.[244] Homelessness is not just a problem in cities across America; homeless people can be found in small towns and rural areas as well. Included within this group are those who are struggling with various mental health issues and have no resources to fund their treatment. The needs of the poor arising in American communities require a radical change in the church's focus and approach.

The Hedonists – These are people who believe and feel that the most important pursuit for their lives is pleasure. Hedonists are often labeled pleasure-seekers.[245] This group of people lives for themselves, dealing with the pressures of life by partying at every possible opportunity. Coping with the realities of life is just too painful to deal with, so this group escapes by filling every moment with activities that will anaesthetize their pain.[246] Though some may be adopting the prevailing values of society, others are taking advantage of the increased permissiveness of the culture as they grasp the opportunity to make their own choices and assert their own rights. Hedonists are grasping for happiness any way they can in the midst of their personal traumas and fragmented, broken family backgrounds.[247]

The Traditionalists – This title can be deceiving since there are others who group people under this heading. Though Drane calls this group traditionalists, his definition is somewhat different than the mainstream. For Drane, traditionalists are defined and understood by the local communities in which they live, where they work and play, and the values they share among the people with whom they associate. Fundamentally, this group is happy, and there is not a lot they would change in their world. Though Drane classifies them as conservative, they are not to be defined by today's theological or political position of what a conservative is. For Drane, this group of conservatives are defined by their families; they live for their immediate surroundings and value a sense of continuity within the context of their world—in their neighborhoods, schools, cafes, local shopping and eateries, and churches. The locality determines detailed differences among this group, and they live for their immediate surroundings.[248] Politicians and church leaders easily misunderstand this group. Traditionalists can appear conservative socially and morally, and they can look like fundamentalists, but in reality, their values are derived from the circumstances of family life.[249] Traditionalists are not normally drawn to the church due to church programs but due to a personal message of faith spoken from the heart of the speaker.[250]

The Spiritual Searchers – This group is characterized by a desire for self-fulfillment. The postmodern culture affords them the opportunity to accomplish their search. Though this group may identify what they search for, it is the search itself that is the all-important thing to them.[251] Spiritual searchers identify themselves as those who try to find meaning for their lives, and they often proudly list the different religions and philosophies embraced in their search. Though holding a smorgasbord of beliefs, spiritual searchers are content to remain no closer to the truth and to continue searching. They ironically feel somehow satisfied in an endless process of exploring diverse ideas and do not possess a desire to settle on any one of those ideas.

Drane shares a story of an encounter that he and his wife had one afternoon with an older man who he describes as having a classic postmodernity mindset. In the course of the conversation, the older man stated, "I think we really need to put reason in its place and live more directly from the heart. Rationality is good for making grocery lists so you don't forget things, but it's a very bad guide to relationships, and even worse for the spiritual life."[252] The point is, the postmodernity mindset is not limited to the younger generations but extends to all who are open to its philosophical beliefs.

The spiritual searchers are the largest group within America. They are the movers and shakers within our communities; they are the organizers of campaigns and petitions. This group does not see our inherited institutions working effectively. For the same reason, this group will not be attracted to the church. These spiritual searchers see the church filled with too much religion and too little genuine spirituality. Church for this group is more than just a gathering that meets one or two times a week. These individuals seek a more holistic approach to spirituality. Christians will protest this misunderstanding of what the church is supposed to be; however, searchers see little evidence of the radical lifestyle for everyday living within the church. Church no longer works for them, it is irrelevant, and it no longer speaks their language. And yet, if the church can see what they value, learn to connect to them, and demonstrate that Christianity really is a radical change of lifestyle to be lived out every day, not just Sunday or whatever day they meet, the church could reach these spiritual searchers.[253]

The Corporate Achievers – The people in this group are dominated by their careers. Though corporate achievers are career-minded, they do not see corporate achievement as the goal for life. This group of achievers would abandon their predictable careers in order to enhance other important areas in their lives like relationships. These individuals find their true identity through family connections and in the local community. Driven for success, this group can find themselves living beyond their means in order to maintain their image of success. However, few truly reach success even by their own standards, so this group finds itself feeling more genuinely lonely, living a fragmented lifestyle, having little self-worth, and lacking individual identity.

What distinguishes this group from the Spiritual Searchers—though both groups may find themselves in the same types of professional employment—is that the corporate achiever will internalize the value of the marketplace engendered by culture. In other words, their value is assigned to what they do, not who they are. The individual who buys into this philosophy of "marketplace value" is grounded in winning and getting to the top, even at the expense of personal relationships falling apart. Relationships are built around each party having the same kind of viewpoint on life. Achievers find relationships difficult because they possess a tendency to view people in terms of the opportunity that they present to market a product. Achievers struggle with personal life and public life because they tend to value people who accept their worldview.[254] The spiritual searcher would not internalize the marketplace value this way.

The Secularists – This group is relatively small, though American culture is often categorized by churches as being secular and humanistic. This group is less likely to respond to the gospel; however, they are extremely influential, and Drane describes them as "a globalized elite culture."[255] The secularists are generally individuals with a "higher education, academics and other high-flying professionals."[256] Therefore, this group manages to maneuver into positions allowing them tremendous influence over the West's educational system, the media, and certain sections of government, thus permitting them to define reality. Also, the secularists still hold to and defend the liberal beliefs of Enlightenment. In their worldview, the secularization thesis states that the progress of modernity will inevitably annihilate spirituality.[257]

Secularist influence has served to distract American churches. Because churches have expended energy to try and appease this group of people, the one-sided emphasis has left Western churches ill-equipped to address the culture's new popular emphasis on spirituality. Secularism has engendered a perception that the church has nothing to offer society.[258]

The Apathetic – This group may represent a significant number of people. This is not to be taken in a negative sense but there are people who "do not give any thought to the bigger issues connected with meaning and identity."[259] These individuals live life centered on trivialities, meaning they live life through a set of routines and structures that cannot be interrupted. An apathetic person has a weekly pattern fixed in such a way that even if there is much free time, he or she cannot break that routine, for it would disrupt a preferred way of life. These individuals value keeping busy and occupied. This group of people might be superstitious, but that is the closest they will come to any type of spirituality.[260]

These seven categories do not exhaust all that might be said about the change occurring in Western culture. Also, there is not a strict line of demarcation between each grouping, for some overlap. The point is that people are not imprisoned in the social class of their birth, nor are they held to certain outlooks on life. Also, this grouping should help the Church understand the challenges they face trying to reach such diverse groups of people.[261]

Another important fact that emerges from Drane's group definitions is that most of the people attending contemporary churches are traditionalists and corporate achievers. The hedonists, the desperately poor, and the secularists are virtually never there or have just excluded themselves. This is not only a reflection of the traditional churches but independent churches as well.[262]

Six Negative Perceptions

Another set of barriers can possibly prevent people from attending church. Sometimes cultural issues arise, and cultural changes occur in the community, and if a church takes a stand or addresses any of these issues, the church only affirms negative perceptions the younger generation already had. These negative perceptions are often the reasons some people refuse to attend church, sometimes even openly expressing their dissatisfaction based on some of the following undesirable views. Though some of these perceptions in the following list have always existed, recent American culture has birthed new ones the church must face. These six negative perceptions are the following:

Hypocritical – In light of the shift occurring in America's culture, any moral stand can communicate a morally superior, judgmental, and/or intolerant attitude. The younger generation and those outside[263] the church may think of churchgoers as being unreal.[264] As an example, a young couple who grew up in the church and who were strong believers abstained from sex before marriage. Some of their peers refused to believe that this young couple kept themselves morally pure before marriage. The belief was that no one could keep from pre-marital sex. Thus, the outsiders, the peers, thought the couple who said they waited until they were married to have sex were lying and hypocritical.

Unfortunately, double standards and unchristian behavior by those who claim to be Christian only reinforce the idea that Christians are polished in their image, but this does not accurately reflect who they are. Regrettably, many of the younger generations and outsiders see church as the place for Christians to play the part of a virtuous and morally pure person.[265]

Too focused on getting converts – No one wants to be considered just a number or a prize to be won. The church's focus on reaching the lost comes across that the unsaved are just another notch to be accounted for and conveys the idea that the church does not really care. This also causes the younger generation and outsiders to question the church's motives.[266]

Homophobic – Christians are considered bigots because of their treatment of the LGBTQ community. Instead of reaching out in love, the church has been focused more on trying to cure the homosexual and work for political legislation against them.[267]

Sheltered – The church is perceived as antiquated, not connected with reality, and boring. The younger generation and outsiders look at the church as being too simplistic and not willing to deal with the real issues, to get involved with the grit and grime of people's lives.[268]

Too political – The younger generation and outsiders do not pick Jesus as one of the top famous Christian people. When a survey taken of young churchgoers, even the President George W. Bush beat out Jesus as one of the top famous Christian people; the point is that the younger generation and outsiders think Christians are overly motivated by a political agenda that is clearly conservative.[269] A conservative position makes Christians "right-wingers."[270]

Judgmental[271] – This is a perception that works against the church's message of love more than any other. Dealing with sin and lifestyles that are opposed to the life of Christ only heightens the perception that the church is judgmental.

These six perceptions create a complex belief system necessitating that the church work toward a breakthrough to reach the younger and lost generations. In addition, these six perceptions were not formed in a vacuum but are the result of a wide range of experiences. The reason this is so significant is that the church holds some responsibility for what the younger generation believes. The blame lies not only with those who oppose the church but also with the church itself.

A young man who was a grad student from the University of California—Berkeley, exemplifies this point. Talking to the pastor one day after visiting a church, he said, "I go to some churches, and they talk a lot about Jesus but little about the world. I go to other churches, and they talk a lot about the world but little about Jesus. ... I know a lot of people like me ... I want to know, if I hang out at your church, will I meet people who are really like Jesus?"[272] It does not take research to understand that today outsiders feels the church resembles little of the One they claim to follow.[273]

Chapter 7

Barriers or Connectors?

Normally, the difference existing between generations is not seen as a value but as a problem that needs to be overcome.²⁷⁴ Consider the generations as living in "different countries"²⁷⁵ or different cultures. One cannot assume that those born in America share the same set of characteristics, grown up being educated the same way, speaking English, and having the same goals and expectations. That is simply not true. Some actions, styles of communication, worldviews, mannerisms, and personality traits communicate something different than what the one communicating intends. When one is seeking to connect, knowledge of such differences is critical. Looking through the lens of a typical traditionalist, the younger generation may appear to lack concern, have poor work ethics, and be lazy. Those with this perspective may not be able to make sense of why the younger generations cannot fit into their worldview and expectations. The problem compounds as each generation views the other generations with suspicion, wondering what the other group's problem is and why the other generation will not meet their expectations.

The differences create barriers, which prevent connection. However, the very areas that create barriers can possibly become "sticking points"²⁷⁶ for building relationships (i.e., helping people "stick together"). One positive way the younger generation influences the church today is their approach to diversity and multiculturalism.[277] Anna Liotta states that a need to understand generational codes is important for relational dynamics.[278] Shaw lists twelve points that can assist people to avoid the tensions that often create barriers:[279]

Communication – If churches are going to keep the mission on track, decoding communication and learning to understand others is critical.[280] This also means churches are going to have to get familiar with the tools the younger generations use.[281] Liotta states that not only the younger generation has a preferred style for communicating, but each generation has their own preferred style for communicating.[282] What makes communication difficult between the generations is that the Millennials and Gen Zs or Nexters, as Liotta calls them, use bits and bytes for communicating their whole lives; it is natural to them.[283] It is suggested by some research that leaders should utilize a variety of styles of communication in order to become better and more effective leaders.[284]

Decision-making – Issues need to be openly discussed with all involved and all feeling their ideas are respected. All generations want to have input in the decisions that will impact their lives, work, and families, and they want to know that the decision was made fairly.[285]

Dress Code – The real issue for discussion on a dress code is the image the organization wishes to communicate to those outside of the organization.[286] The younger generations do not value dress codes as the older generation does. However, the importance on dress comes from advice by another Millennial who stated, "Remember that everything you do, wear, and say WILL be judged. Do everything you can to act with integrity and make a good impression on your coworkers."[287]

Feedback – Providing good feedback means that the generations need to discuss what feedback means to each group and how often each group would like to receive feedback.[288]

Fun – Fun is important to Millennials because they want to make personal friends at work. A normal day at work that does not provide some opportunity for social time for building relationships and a bit of humor will not engage Millennials. As a matter of fact, each generation wants some time for socializing, building relationships, and having some fun.[289] In addition, Millennials have played electronic games, attended sophisticated technological amusement parks, and they cannot remember not having a computer or access to a computer.[290] Both GenXers and Millennials do not understand why work cannot be fun. This is due to the fact that both generations saw their parents come home exhausted and stressed from the demands of work.[291]

Knowledge Transfer – This sticking point focuses on the previous generation passing on knowledge to those who are younger than them. This involves mentoring and coaching others as well as providing structured data that could be resourced by someone needing information to accomplish needed tasks within the organization.[292]

Loyalty – Loyalty is important but has different definitions to each generation. It is also important to clarify how loyalty fits the present economic and work reality. Additionally, a shift must occur away from criticizing other generations' definitions of loyalty and toward focusing energy on ways to support each group working better together so all generations remain to fulfill the vision and mission of the organization.[293]

Meetings – This is a popular arena for conflict among the generations, or this can be a strong sticking point that helps people "stick" together. The struggle lies in making meetings interesting so all the generations will engage, communicate, and connect as a team. This requires a willingness from each generation to understand the other generation's view on the importance and frequency of meetings.[294] Learning to lead good meetings allows for generations to respect

Facilitating Change to Reach All Generations

others and build trust.[295]

Policies – Two approaches exist to making polices in organizations: (1) developing policies from the top down, which is the default of managing and not leading, and (2) engaging each generation by allowing individuals from each group to form a committee for the purpose of coming up with recommendations of policies. This is a leadership approach.[296]

Respect – A foundational point for many of the other sticking points, working through this one point will either intensify the stress and conflict among the organization or help it become stronger as colleagues work through the different definitions of respect. Everyone wants to be heard and feel that he or she has a voice in what matters.[297] However, each generation is unique in their views and all generations have these two fundamental things in common that can become a barrier to work through. First, all generations believe they see the world correctly, and second, each generation wants all the other generations to respect how they see the world.[298]

Training – Each generation wants the kind of training that will help them keep up with the world that is changing. However, their desire is for training that works and is not boring. The key is open conversations on the particular issues needing to be addressed, along with appropriate training to aid each generation involved to communicate together.[299] Something that needs to be considered is that there are sometimes five different generations learning, each on their own level with their own style for learning. This difference in learning styles creates challenges every organization is struggling with.[300] Some of the challenges go beyond style; each generation has their own attitudes and expectations toward learning.[301]

Work ethics – In a world that is 24/7, organizations are learning how to accomplish work on different levels. Each organization needs to figure out how to measure the work that needs to be completed.[302] Creating a work environment that supports freedom for creativity, to improvise, to not feel threatened if failure occurs, and employees are not underestimated produces workplace satisfaction.303

These twelve points provide information on the areas that could be sticking points that cause a team or church to become stuck or become areas for generations to stick together. The younger generations get their identity, value, and their sense of belonging more from their associations and relationships than they do from the institution they serve. The goal is to position the church to take advantage of the differences existing among the generations rather than to allow those differences to divide.304

Conclusion to Section Two

Section Two's purpose was to discover possible issues causing a church's inability to connect with the younger generations of people. The first issue that emerged from this review began with a certain naiveté that exists among leaders and influencers at times. The issue does not simply rest with wrong information the younger generation acquire or that they simply need fixing by finding the right program or vehicle that allows the church to travel into their world, correct all their misconceived information, and then lead them to the Promised Land. The issues are far more complex, needing definite solutions and answers that adequately address the problems in love. A church cannot change the culture of its community, but it can change its own culture within the church so it welcomes and receive all generations.

There are real issues that need addressing and barriers that need tearing down. Understanding the shift in America's culture and how that culture is impacting everything, including the Church, is necessary for building the right context for reaching the younger generations and outsiders. Taking the time to learn not just the differences existing between the generations but also understanding the different kinds of people attending church and the different types of people in our communities will help each church to demonstrate genuine concern and compassion for people.

Negative perceptions of the church already exist, but leaders and congregants can take steps to overcome those negative views. The younger generation is looking for the real and authentic Church, a group of people living the gospel and demonstrating God's genuine love in a broken world. Some of the steps churches can take are to make sure they do not ignore the younger generation nor try to fix them or make deals that really do not accomplish the purpose of vision and mission of the church.

Churches face enormous challenges to passing on faith to the younger generations and reaching others outside the church community. Churches struggle with navigating the technological, spiritual, and social changes that define the times. With questions arising about authority and increasing relational and institutional estrangement, today's Church is going to have to learn how to present a faith worth claiming.

SECTION THREE

Section Three provides resources for addressing the growing challenge of reaching all generations. It is vital that church leaders gain insight into the specific challenges they face in their particular ministry environment in order to gain direction for the best way forward. Though understanding the differences between the generations is important, it is just as important to understand that America's culture has changed permanently from the modern culture, which was strongly influenced by Christianity and the Church, to a postmodern culture; in fact, some even argue we are now in a post-postmodern culture. An understanding of the culture lays the foundation for helping each leader and church connect with all generations.

The following chapters contain material developed for the Living Word seminar: the seminar agenda and session description overview, and a Facilitator's Guide, and a pre-post assessment instrument to evaluate learning and gain feedback on the quality of the presentation and presenter. Should you wish to evaluate your teaching or study session, you may adapt this assessment tool for your given context. I also developed a Participant's Guide and PowerPoint/media presentation, but those are not included in this book.

Chapter 8
Seminar Agenda and Session Overview

For a one-day seminar format, the following sample provides a suggested agenda for presenting the material discussed in this book.

Seminar Agenda

8:00   Refreshments, Greetings, and Prayer

8:30   Distribution of Pre-Assessment
- Answering of Any Questions Regarding the Pre-Assessment
- Distribution of Materials for the Day

9:00   First Session
- Defining the Generations
- Characteristics of the Different Generations

9:50   Break

10:00 Second Session
- Three Kinds of People in Church
- The Different Kinds of People the Church Needs to Reach
- Why Is It So Hard to Reach People Today?

10:50 Break

11:00 Third Session
- What is Culture?
- The Shift in Our Culture
  - Modern, Postmodern
  - Secular Humanism

12:00 Lunch

12:40 Fourth Session
- How Culture Has Affected the Generations
- Worldview

1:30   Break

1:40   Fifth Session
- The Original Design
- The Fall

- God's Intervention
- God's Cultural Project – Part 1

2:30 Break

2:40 Sixth Session
- God's Cultural Project – Part 2

3:30 Break

3:40 Seventh Session
- Jesus the Cultural Cultivator
- The Greatest Cultural Event in History
- Pentecost to the Present

4:30 Break

4:40 Conclusion

4:50 Wrap-up
- Post-Assessment

5:00 Closing and Prayer

The Seven Sessions—An Overview

Following this initial overview, in the following chapter, is the full Facilitator's Guide. This Guide can serve as a resource for teaching the material of this book as a seminar, sermon series, or adapting it for small group settings.

Each session, except for the first, can open with a Scripture reading. The first session's opening statement phrases the Scripture to emphasize that every believer is responsible to perpetuate the name of the Lord to all generations forever (Ps 45:17). This is a directive for believers, not a suggestion. Once the goals are covered for the day, you might share a couple of introductory thoughts:

- Each generation is influenced by the previous generation, positively or negatively.
- Major decisions made by one generation have shaped culture affecting the next generation.

Session One

Session one's first point defines the six generations presently living in America and emphasizes the four generations actively working, competing, and colliding in the marketplace and in church.

As characteristics of the generations are covered briefly, questions may continue to arise. Individuals may start to have "aha" moments as they realize the importance of understanding the difference between generations.

Session Two

Session two addresses three categories of Christians: cultural Christians, congregational Christians, and convictional Christians.[305] Also discussed in this session are the seven distinct groups of people who the Church needs to be aware of reaching: the desperate poor, the hedonists, the traditionalists, the spiritual searchers, the corporate achievers, the secularists, and the apathetic. These seven categories do not exhaust all that might be said about the change occurring in America's culture. Traditional values of the church are not embraced by our culture as a whole; nor are the traditional methodologies of churches reaching most of these people in the seven categories.

Session Three

Research from *unChristian*, written by David Kinnaman and Gabe Lyons, indicates that outsiders and unchurched people view modern-day Christianity as no longer being Christian. To Kinnaman's and Lyons's surprise, their research uncovered a growing hostility toward Christians. Outsiders feel they perceive clearly what Christians stand against, even sensing that Christians are angry, violent, and illogical.

You could open the third session with those comments and then shift the focus to culture.

The Western/modern culture of America contrasts starkly with the postmodern culture that America has become. After you clearly describe the postmodern culture, you can conclude this lesson by defining secular humanism. Secular humanism is broader than atheism, for atheism concerns itself only with the nonexistence of God or the supernatural.

Session Four

Session four moves from the particular point of culture influencing everything in life to focusing on worldviews. The research from Barna is staggering when considering the dismal fact that only nine percent of those who claim to be born-again believers hold to a biblical worldview.

A worldview frames one's belief system—how one views reality and makes sense of life and the world. You might offer a brief quiz in this session to allow each participant to measure their personal worldview components.

Session Five

With this session, the seminar shifts toward the biblical-theological point of view providing the biblical foundation of God's design for culture. From the beginning of Creation, the Lord intended humanity to develop and live in culture. God set the foundation, laying the groundwork from the start when He "planted a garden in the east, in Eden; and there he put the man he had formed" (Gen 2:8). God's design established the beliefs, the parameters that humanity would live in, the directives for living together, and the goals for humanity (1:26-28; 2:15-18, 23-25).

Adam and Eve failed to keep the culture God established for them, resulting in a counterculture that now runs against the values and beliefs of the Lord. However, God had a plan to intervene in humanity's lostness: I refer to this plan as God's "Cultural Project." The Lord chose to begin His project with the selection of Abraham and his decedents.

Session Six

Session six picks up with the conclusion of the Cultural Project. The first point also finishes the discussion about the values of this culture. The focus is on the name of the Lord, "I AM WHO I AM" (Exod 3:14). Yahweh is the name that God chose to reveal to Moses and the children of Israel. Yahweh is God's only personal name; all the rest are titles. This revelation is being renewed with God officially calling Moses and giving His personal name.

This session also covers the presentation of the Ten Commandments given at the Mountain of God. What is unique here is that God spoke the Ten Commandments to the entire nation, not to Moses alone on the mountain (Exod 20:1-17).

At the end of this session is the transition of leadership from Moses to Joshua. As this session unfolds, the participants learn that Joshua was Moses's aid. Moses included Joshua in certain personal encounters that he had with God. This created a desire in Joshua for the presence of God (Exod 33:11).

Session Seven

The seventh session moves from the Old Testament to the New and focuses on the fulfillment of the prophetic hope, the coming Messiah, who is the ultimate culture maker.

Jesus did not just pass on Israel's cultural inheritance, though the early years of His life were spent learning and living the culture of His people. The important idea here is that Jesus lived out His divinity in a normal life as a young Jewish adult in Nazareth. The One who created all of heaven and earth lived out His early life as an ordinary person, not concealing His divinity. As this session continues, the focus is on what Jesus brought to culture when He started ministry.

Jesus suffered the full weight of humanity's sin and rebellion against God. As important as the Cross is, the greatest cultural event in history is the resurrection. It is the resurrection that has changed more cultures and more people than any other event in history.

The session then turns to the book of Acts, beginning with the Day of Pentecost and quickly moving through the rest of Acts, leaving the ending open. The story that unfolds in Acts is one about cities. Like bookends, the story begins in Jerusalem and ends in Rome. In between these two bookends are stops along the way, touching just about every commercial and political center around the Mediterranean Sea. Almost all of the activity of the gospel moving through the empire took place in urban centers. Hence,

Facilitating Change to Reach All Generations

Acts is also about culture.

Some people you are presenting this material to may never have considered the idea that God had created culture for humanity.

I recommend that you end all of the sessions with some questions to provide further dialogue on the topic covered and ensure that you leave plenty of time to address those questions.

The Facilitator's Guide in the next chapter provides more in-depth content for the seven teaching sessions.

Chapter 9
Facilitator's Guide

Facilitator's Guide

First Session

The Bible instructs us to perpetuate the name of the Lord to all generations so that the nations will praise His name forever (Ps 45:17).

Today's goal is to provide you with some helpful information on the generations and their differences, culture, worldview, the different kinds of people we are trying to reach, barriers we face, and the bad press against the church.[306]

I want to begin with some introductory thoughts.

- Each generation is influenced by the previous generation, positively or negatively.
- Major decisions made by one generation have shaped culture while also affecting the next generation.

Defining Generations

What is a generation?

A. A generation is a group of people born and living around the same time period or a group of people belonging to a specific category. There are six generations living in America; four of those are actively working, buying and selling, competing, and colliding in the marketplace and in church. The four prominent generations at this time are the Traditionalists, Boomers, Generation X, and Generation Y or Millennials. We hear a lot about Millennials right now. The first group of Generation Z or Boomlets is just beginning to emerge and come of age.

The following provides a brief look at the characteristics of the five generations.

B. Characteristics of the Generations

1. The Traditionalists, born before 1945, are also called the Builders, and include the G.I. Generation, the Mature/Silents, and the War Babies.

    a) The youngest Traditionalists still exert enormous influence on the organizations they built, which in turn is influencing culture.[307] The Great Depression and World Wars I and II shaped this generation. Traditionalists learned to sacrifice and show patience. They had saved the world, and then they came home and built a nation.[308]

    b) Traditionalists had more confidence in leaders and large organizations because they witnessed how the large hierarchical organization could get things done.[309] They in turn built strong hierarchical organizations using what they learned, a command-and-control approach.[310]

    c) This generation was made up of doers who were assertive, loyal, had a strong work ethic, were excellent team players, and kept their jobs for life. They saw marriage as a lifelong commitment, viewed having children out of wedlock as unacceptable, and were avid readers.[311] There was a rapid migration from the farm to the city with this generation.[312]

2. Baby Boomers, born between 1946 and 1964, were trained and educated by the Traditionalists during the time that America was growing, building, and prosper-ing. It was the best of times, marked by hope, opportu-nity, and the feeling that things would get better.[313] "Boomers grew up as the most optimistic generation in"[314] the history of America.

   a) Communities were not ready for the explosion of growth that occurred across the country. Hospitals did not have enough beds; schools were not prepared for the number of students enrolling, and colleges and universities did not have enough faculty or living space.[315] This overcrowding and lack of space created an atmosphere of compete-tion. Boomers were taught to compete to get what they wanted. This meant that everyone made the Little League team, but only the best got to play.[316]

   b) The Boomers "grew up in the most economically optimistic times in"[317] American history; they changed the "value system from sacrifice to self."[318] Affluence explains the Boomers' distinctive values; "affluence funded the focus on self and the optimism that made the Boomers' growing-up years magical."[319] Boomers were told they were special; thus the "me" generation was born.[320] Boomers were the first generation to have the influence of TV. In 1963 when John F. Kennedy "was assassinated, it was said that it was the first time the nation cried together."[321] Television brought the images of Kennedy's assassination to every corner of the country.[322]

   c) The move from the farm to the suburbs created a subculture—the teenager. "Before World War II, the word teenager was"[323] seldom used, because teens were just considered a younger version of adults.

After World War II, marketers saw the profit of this younger generation who were not interested in buying their parents' fashions and focused on appealing to this emerging generation.[324]

d) Along with this newly arising subculture emerged a generation gap. With the Traditionalists' ability to provide the American dream, they could not believe the drop in educational achievement and the rise in drug use, teen pregnancies, and crime. Home was competing with the influences of teachers and the media. The Traditionalists could not believe that their values were undercut by the education system, creating a gap with their kids.[325]

e) Boomers were the first generation who considered divorce acceptable and who began accepting homosexuality.[326] There are three significant shifts in values among Boomers. The first is a moral value—"sex, authority, religion, and obligation to others;"[327] the second shift was in social values—"money, work, family, and marriage;"[328] and the third was self-fulfillment. Boomers moved from sacrifice to self-fulfillment creating the "me" generation. Also, the Boomers were the first generation "to have the money, time, and freedom to explore self and search for meaning."[329]

f) The oldest and the youngest Boomers had different experiences and opportunities. The older Boomers had more in common with Traditionalists, came of age with the optimism and idealism of the Kennedy years, and reveled in the success of the space program.[330] The younger Boomers had more in common with Generation X. This group of Boom-ers grew up with Watergate and the Arab oil embargo, and they lacked the same optimism as their older predecessors.[331]

3. The next group is called Generation X, born between 1965

and 1980. The metaphor that one author used to describe this generation is Donkey Kong, the video game. The game symbolizes the challenges that this generation had to overcome.[332] Considered the "latch-key kids," they grew up street-smart but were isolated. The term "latch-key kids" came from the key children carried or wore around their necks so they could let themselves into an empty house or apartment after school.[333]

a) They often had to deal with divorce or career-driven parents.[334] The Gen Xers faced multiple recessions, global competition, and the rising tide of missing children whose pictures ended up on milk cartons. Gen Xers became realists as they coped with life's never-ending challenges, learned to roll with the bad news, and realized they did not want to dedicate themselves to the game of life like Boomers. The result was that Boomers misunder-stood the Gen Xers, saw them as cynical whiners and called them slackers in the workplace.[335]

b) "As open-eyed realists, it made no sense to the Gen Xers to keep the same high expectation as if the world had not changed."[336] Not only had the world changed, it was continuing to evolve, moving from the moorings of the Traditionalists and Boomers. The Gen Xers were not slackers; they were just rewriting the game or world they inherited, and they were beginning to do it with new technology and with new expectations. "Get real" was the phrase the Gen Xers embraced to challenge the older generations to stop trying to spin that everything would be ok, that it would have a happy ending.[337]

c) Gen Xers are entrepreneurial and very individualistic; government and big business mean little to them. They want to save their neighborhood, not the world. They were raised in a time when society was transitioning from the analog world to the digital world. Many remember starting school without computers, but before graduating high school, computers were being introduced as tools for learning.

d) Gen Xers are eager to make their relationships work, and they want to be there for their kids. They want to have a chance to contribute, to learn, and explore, but Gen Xers tend to be committed to self rather than a specific career or an organization. One looming cloud for Gen Xers was the rise and spread of AIDS.[338]

e) Gen Xers are skeptical. The confidence in the economy went bust for them, and the American dream was downsized. Many "Gen Xers began their adult life with unprecedented personal debt"[339] from college as expenses quadrupled, and grants and other aids were slashed. Though they were pessimistic and suspicious, three out of four Gen Xers were ambitious and wanted to succeed. They were the first generation to question the story behind the story on their computers and to feel that the news would always be shaded by someone's perspective. In other words, Gen Xers believed that you could not believe everything you are told.[340]

4. Generation Y, also called Millenniums or Millennials, were born between 1981 and 2000. They are also known as "The 9/11 Generation,"[341] the second Baby Boom,[342] America's next great generation.[343]

a) Millennials have an attitude that treats others the way they get treated. They will ignore those who ignore them.[344] They also expect to be taken seriously, even though they do not have any "real-world" experience.[345] After nine months on a job, Millennials get bored and then act like it is their Gen Xer manager's problem, and Shaw states, "it is" their problem. Gen Xers and Boomers are responsible for teaching Millennials to think this way.[346]

b) The difference between the parents of Millennials and Boomers is that Millennial parents hovered over their children nurturing them. The president of Wake Forest University called these parents "helicopter parents" due to their constant involvement and oversight. Parents actually became more like activities directors as they arranged and managed play dates, soccer games, ballet, swim team, music lessons, and anything else their Millennial children wanted to do. When Millennials grew to college age, their parents were just part of the package.[347]

c) A huge contrast exists between Boomers and Millennials. Millennials saw their parents as an assist, and they would seek advice from them regularly. Boomers felt they did not need their parents and saw them as part of the establishment. Millennials not only saw their parents as a resource for everyday life issues, they sought out their parents to help them when it came to work. It would not be unusual for employers to have Millennial parents tag along with their children for a job interview.[348] Shaw provided this advice for employers if the parents walked in for the interview with their children: "engage them."[349]

d) Millennials are confident, encouraged to express their feelings, and raised as consumers. Their parents worked to shield their self-esteem. There were no losers, and everyone received a trophy for participating.[350] They are the first generation to not know what it is not to have a computer, a phone, the Internet, and Google at their fingertips. The world to a Millennial is a 24/7 place in which one can just about get anything desired, access everyone's information, and connect socially with anyone through the Internet. Millennials do not live to work but prefer an environment that is very relaxed, complete with open communication, support, and accolades. They are less loyal to their jobs than previous generations.[351]

C. The current generation is known as Generation Z or the Boomlets. The people of this were born after 2001.

   1. Generation Z will change the behavior and culture of America. This is because in 2006, the number of Gen Z births outnumbered the start of the Baby Boomers, 49 percent were Hispanic, and they will easily grow to be the largest generation in American history.[352]

   2. Also, the Gen Zs will be the most technologically advanced group in the history of America. Most have televisions in their rooms, video games, DVD players, and their own cell phones.[353]

   3. They have never known a world that did not have computers or smart phones. With computers and web-based learning, this generation is leaving behind their toys at a much younger age.[354]

   4. The Gen Zs are more aware of the advantages of the web and computers; therefore, they are savvy consumers, knowing what they want and how to get it. This generation is oversaturated with information from every angle: Internet, web TV, Netflix, Amazon, Google, and a variety of social media options.[355]

Do you think understanding the differences between the generations is important?

Where there any surprises regarding the information?

Did this information help you?

Second Session

"I will sing of the LORD's great love forever; with my mouth I will make your faithfulness known through all generations" (Ps 89:1).

This second session will look at the three kinds of people who attend church, the seven different groups of people the Church needs to reach, and why it is hard to reach people today.

I. Three Kinds of People

The change that is occurring in America is affecting the church's culture as well. The contemporary church finds itself dealing within three different categories of Christians:[356]

- A. Cultural Christians – these are people who believe they are Christians because their culture tells them they are, that is – through Christian heritage. These particular individuals may have religious roots or come from a group of people are tied to a certain denomination, like Southern evangelicals or Irish Catholics. The individuals in this category are Christian in name only, not practicing a vibrant faith.[357]

- B. Congregational Christians – similar to the first group, except these individuals at least have some connection to congregational life. This group has a home church they grew up in and possibly they were even married in their church. This group is called attendees, visiting occasionally but they are not practicing any sort of real, vibrant faith.[358]

- C. Convictional Christians – this group is actually living according to their faith. The final group are people who have given their lives over to Jesus. Their lives are marked with change, not perfection. The people of this group would say their lives have been increasingly oriented around the life of Jesus and their faith in Him.[359]

Which category do you fit into? **(Do not answer, just asking to challenge you.)**

What do you think is our responsibility toward the first two categories?

What is our responsibility toward the last category?

D. Part of our job as the Church is to help people move from the first category to the last category. It is our goal to help individuals experience the reality of Jesus, so they willingly want to grow from a cultural Christian to a fully devoted follower of Jesus Christ.

1. It is important that as church leaders and influencers, we step into the position of <u>NOT</u> judging those we see but step into <u>HELPING</u> them see their need of having a vibrant relationship with Jesus.

2. We do not know the journey that people are on. What is clear that there are a whole lot of people using the self-identification of Christian who are not living like fully devoted disciples of Jesus.

II. **Different Kinds of People**

- There are seven distinct groups of people within our community. We need to look beyond the generations and see the people that we need to relate to if we are going to fulfill the church's missional mandate.[360]

- Our missional mandate is our vision: Helping people to become fully devoted followers of Jesus Christ. It is fulfilling the Great Commission.

- The seven distinct groups are: the desperate poor, the hedonists, the traditionalists, the spiritual searchers, the corporate achievers, the secularists, and the apathetic.

- These seven categories do not exhaust all the groups that exist within our culture, nor is there a strict demarcation between each group.[361] What this means is that these seven groups

Facilitator's Guide

are not identified necessarily by age, political preference, economics, or gender and race.

- One of the main points of this kind of information is to provide awareness that our culture is more openly diverse than the church is generally willing to accept. In addition, this information exposes the overall centrality in which the church ministers; churches are reaching people just like themselves or just certain kinds of people.

- The traditional values of the church are not embraced by our culture as a whole, nor are the traditional methodologies of churches reaching the people. "A more useful way of understanding people in relation to the mission of the church will be to try and identify how they are dealing with the rationalization and apparent meaninglessness of life."[362] This is more of a cultural and missiological analysis.

A. Below is a brief definition of each group that the church will need to relate to if it seeks to fulfill the Great Commission mandate:

1. The Desperate Poor – One of the rapid changes that have occurred within our culture is the dramatic increase in the number of people living in poverty. The gap is widening between those who have and those who have not.[363]

   a) Homelessness is not just a problem in cities across America; homeless people can be found in small towns and rural areas as well.[364]

   b) According to Maryland's Homeless Management Information Systems, 981 homeless people reside in the area surrounding Living Word Community Church.[365]

   Think about that number. Almost one thousand people are homeless living around us right now.

   c) The Mission, a local outreach group says that the number is in reality much higher than the stats provided by the state. The needs of the poor arising in American communities require a radical change in the church's focus and approach.

2. The Hedonists – How many here know what this word means? A hedonist is a person who believes that the pursuit of pleasure is the most important thing in life. Hedonists are often labeled pleasure-seekers.[366]

   a) This group of people lives for themselves, dealing with the pressures of life by partying at every possible opportunity.[367]

   b) Coping with the realities of life is just too painful to deal with, so this group escapes by filling every moment with activities that will anaesthe-tize their pain.[368]

   c) Though some may be adopting the prevailing values of society, others are taking advantage of the increased permissiveness of the culture as they grasp the opportunity to make their own choices and assert their own rights.[369]

   d) Hedonists are grasping for happiness any way they can in the midst of their personal traumas and fragmented, broken family backgrounds.[370]

3. The Traditionalists – This title can be deceiving since there are others who group people under this heading. The definition here is somewhat different than the mainstream.[371]

   a) Traditionalists are defined and understood by the local communities in which they live, where they work and play, and the values they share among the people with whom they associate.[372]

   b) Fundamentally, this group is happy, and there is not a lot they would change in their world. Though Drane classifies them as conservative, they are not to be defined by today's theological or political position of what a conservative is.³⁷³

c) This group revolves around their families; they live for their immediate surroundings and value a sense of continuity within the context of their world, that is in their neighborhoods, schools, cafes, local shopping and eateries, and churches. The locality determines detailed differences among this group, and they live for their immediate surroundings.³⁷⁴

d) Politicians and church leaders easily misunderstand this group. Traditionalists can appear conservative socially and morally, and they can look like fundamentalists, but in reality, their values are derived from the circumstances of family life.³⁷⁵

e) These traditionalists are not normally drawn to the church due to church programs but due to a personal message of faith spoken from the heart of the speaker.³⁷⁶

4. The Spiritual Searchers – This group is characterized by a desire for self-fulfillment. The postmodern culture affords them the opportunity to accomplish their search.³⁷⁷

   a) Though this group may identify what they search for, it is the search itself that is the all-important thing to them.³⁷⁸ Spiritual searchers identify themselves as those who try to find meaning for their lives, and they often proudly list the different religions and philosophies embraced in their search.

      1) Though holding a smorgasbord of beliefs, spiritual searchers are content to remain no closer to the truth and to continue searching. They ironically feel somehow satisfied in an endless process of exploring diverse ideas and

do not possess a desire to settle on any one of those ideas.

b) An example of this is with an older man in the park one day who has a classic postmodernity mindset. The older man stated, "I think we really need to put reason in its place and live more directly from the heart. Rationality is good for making grocery lists so that you don't forget things, but it's a very bad guide to relationships, and even worse for the spiritual life."[379]

c) The spiritual searchers are the largest group within America. They are the movers and shakers within our communities; they are the organizers of campaigns and petitions. This group does not see our inherited institutions working effectively.[380]

  1) For the same reason, this group will not be attracted to the church. These spiritual searchers see the church filled with too much religion and too little genuine spiritu-ality.[381]

  2) Church for this group is perceived as something that happens once or twice a week, while they seek a holistic approach to spirituality.[382]

  3) Christians will protest this misunderstanding of what the church is supposed to be; however, searchers see little evidence of the radical lifestyle for everyday living.[383]

  4) Church no longer works for them; it is irrelevant, and it no longer speaks their language. And yet, if the church can see what they value, learn to connect to them and demonstrate that Christianity really is a radical change of lifestyle to be lived out every day, not just Sunday or whatever day they meet, the church could reach these spiritual

Facilitator's Guide

searchers.[384]

5. The Corporate Achievers – The people in this group are dominated by their careers. Though corporate achievers are career-minded, they do not see corporate achievement as the goal for life. This group of achievers would abandon their predictable careers in order to enhance other important areas in their lives like relationships.

   a) These individuals find their true identity through family connections and in the local community. Driven for success, this group can find themselves living beyond their means in order to maintain their image of success. However, few truly reach success even by their own standards, so this group finds itself feeling more genuinely lonely, living a fragmented lifestyle, having little self-worth, and lacking individual identity.

   b) What distinguishes this group from the spiritual searchers, though both groups may find themselves in the same types of professional employment, is that the corporate achiever will internalize the value of the marketplace engendered by culture. In other words, their value is assigned to what they do, not who they are.[385]

   c) The individual who buys into this philosophy of "marketplace value" is grounded in winning and getting to the top, even at the expense of personal relationships falling apart. Relation-ships are built around each party having the same kind of viewpoint on life.[386]

   d) Achievers find relationships difficult because they possess a tendency to view people in terms of the opportunity that they present to market a product. Achievers struggle with personal life and public life because they tend to value people who accept their worldview. The spiritual searcher would not internalize the marketplace value this way.[387]

6. The Secularists – This group is relatively small, though the American culture is often categorized by churches as secular humanistic. This group is less likely to respond to the gospel; however, they are extremely influential, and they are known as "a globalized elite culture."[388]

   a) The secularists are generally individuals with a "higher education, academics and other high-flying professionals."[389] Technically, they are the only group left who still self-consciously defend the conventional liberal beliefs of an Enlightenment worldview.[390]

   b) Due to the kind of position this group occupies, they play a large part in determining the official sanctioned definition of reality and meaning reflected in the Western education system, the media, and certain sections of government. In their worldview, the secularization thesis states that the progress of modernity will inevitably annihilate spirituality.

   c) Secularist influence has served to distract American churches. Because churches have expended energy to try to appease this group of people, the one-sided emphasis has left Western churches ill-equipped to address the culture's new popular emphasis on spirituality. Secular-ism has engendered a perception that the church has nothing to offer society.[391]

7. The Apathetic – This group may represent a significant number of people. Many people do not give any thought to the bigger issues connected with meaning and identity.[392] These individuals live life centered on trivialities, meaning they live life through a set of routines and structures that cannot be interrupted.[393]

a) An apathetic person has a weekly pattern fixed in such a way that even if there is a lot of free time, he or she cannot break routine for it would disrupt a preferred way of life. These individuals value keeping busy and occupied. This group of people might be superstitious, but that is the closest they will come to real spirituality.[394]

B. These seven categories do not exhaust all that might be said about the change occurring in Western culture. These individuals are not imprisoned in the social class of their birth, nor are they held to certain outlooks on life. Also, this grouping should help the church understand the challenges they face trying to reach such diverse groups of people.[395]

C. Something important that emerged from my research is that most of the people attending contemporary churches are traditionalists and corporate achievers. The hedonists, the desperately poor, and the secularists are virtually never there or just exclude themselves. This is not just a reflection of the traditional churches but independent churches as well.[396]

As we covered these seven different groups of people, what stood out as unique?

Do you think this information will help you understand the people you are trying to reach?

Did anyone immediately see certain individual/s you know who fit into one or more of these groups?

Third Session

"Now to him who is able to do immeasurably more than all we ask or imagine, according to his power that is at work within us, to him be glory in the church and in Christ Jesus throughout all generations, for ever and ever! Amen" (Eph 3:20-21).

Facilitating Change to Reach All Generations

David Kinnaman and Gabe Lyons wrote a book entitled *unChristian*. Kinnaman and Lyons found that outsiders view modern-day Christianity as no longer being Christian. To Kinnaman's and Lyons's surprise, their research uncovered a growing hostility toward Christians. Outsiders perceive clearly what Christians stand against, even sensing that Christians are angry, violent, and illogical.

What surprises you about the paragraph I just read? How true do you think it is?

I. What Is Culture?

The culture of the United States of America is primarily Western or European in origin and form, though it is influ-enced by the multicultural ethos of the many distinguishing ethnic groups within America.[397]

    A. What is culture? This is how culture is defined:

        1. The cumulative deposit of knowledge, experience, beliefs, values, attitudes, meanings, hierarchies, religion, notions of time, roles, spatial relations, concepts of the universe, and material objects and possessions acquired by a group of people in the course of generations through individual and group striving;[398]

        2. The systems of knowledge shared by a relatively large group of people;[399]

        3. Communication;[400]

        4. Cultivated behavior; that is the totality of a person's learned, accumulated experience, which is socially transmitted, or more briefly, behavior through social learning;[401]

        5. A way of life of a group of people—the behaviors, beliefs, values, and symbols that they accept, generally without thinking about them, and that are passed along by communication and imitation;[402]

        6. Symbolic communication. Some of its symbols include

a group's skills, knowledge, attitudes, values, and motives. The meanings of the symbols are learned and deliberately perpetuated in a society through its institutions;[403]

7. Patterns, explicit and implicit, of and for behavior acquired and transmitted by symbols, constituting the distinctive achievement of human groups, including their embodiments in artifacts; the essential core of culture consists of traditional ideas and especially their attached values; culture systems may, on the one hand, be considered as products of action, and on the other hand, as conditioning influences upon further action;[404]

8. The sum total of the learned behavior of a group of people that is generally considered to be the tradition of that people and that is transmitted from generation to generation;[405]

9. A collective programming of the mind that distinguishes the members of one group or category of people from another.[406]

After covering all this material on culture, what is your first impression about culture?

Does this information help you or just complicate the issue of culture?

B. Let's see if we can simplify this list of descriptive characteristics of culture.

1. First, it should be clear that culture influences everything. Culture even affects the way information is transmitted, the use of time and space, and how authority is viewed.[407]

2. From this list, a working definition of culture is as follows: an aggregate of knowledge, experiences, beliefs, values, attitudes, and behaviors defining and directing a way of life accepted by a group of people.

3. This list also helps to define the church's culture. The church has its own culture that often runs counter to society's culture. This explains why some young unchurched people who walk into a church may feel lost. The church has its own set of values, beliefs, behaviors, symbols, language, forms, and communication that often registers as foreign to the unchurched.

C. While it may be tempting to point a finger to blame the media or some other force for luring the younger generation away from church involvement, this sort of blaming does not really hold to what are the facts.

D. As the American culture has changed, the church itself has reacted in many different ways to those changes. Some of the church's reactions have not welcomed the younger generation. Some church members' actions have likely unintentionally hurt the church's relationship with young newcomers.

E. As an example: on one particular occasion a person in our church chastised a visiting young man who wore his hat into the sanctuary. (This happened several years ago). This visiting young man was an unchurched person who took his hat off but after that service never returned.

What was more important, the hat or the lost soul of that young person?

Do you think your church should have represented Jesus better in this situation?

II. Understanding Culture

The American culture includes the customs and traditions of the United States, which means it also "encompasses religion, food, what we wear, how we wear it, our language, marriage, music, what we believe is right or wrong, how we sit at the table, how we greet visitors, how we behave with loved ones, and a million other things."[408]

A. America combines a plethora of cultures, making understanding the American culture somewhat difficult. Also, the word culture has become the new buzzword in mainstream media, which uses it with a slightly different purpose of promoting an agenda of acceptance and tolerance. This only confuses the meaning of culture, not only in our society but within the church as well.[409]

B. America is the third largest country in the world and one of the most culturally diverse countries in the world. Nearly every region of the world has influenced America's culture; however, America's culture has also influenced the world.

   1. Despite this plethora of cultures existing in America, a prevailing culture influences the country as a whole. Americans live in an increasingly secular and postmodern culture[410] with a growing number of people in communities knowing little of the traditional church.

   2. This lack of knowledge and misunderstanding of the church has in no way prevented people from having a spiritual hunger.[411] The values and attitudes of modernity have been rejected, but that does not mean they have been replaced with another worldview.[412]

   3. Even though countless resources focus on the distinct characteristics of specific age groups and generations, those distinct characteristics are not so self-contained[413] with their particular grouping or generation. As an example, many writers reference the Millennial mindset, which generally refers to people born from 1981 to 2000. The traits of this Millennial way of thinking commonly appear among people identified as Boomers and Gen Xers.

   4. The point is, the issue is more than just a generational issue; it is also cultural. Millennials were not born in a vacuum or with their particular beliefs and values; something or someone is producing and forming the Millennial and Gen Z's worldview and values.

C. Modern

When people talk about Western culture, what exactly are they referring to? Western culture is a broad term used to describe the social norms, belief systems, traditions, customs, values, and so forth that have their origin in Europe or are based on European culture. America, for example, is firmly Western in culture.

1. Another term for "Western Culture" is Modern or Modernity.

    a) The Christian religion is a huge component of Western culture. While not everyone today practices Christianity, the influence of Christianity flows through many fibers of Western/Modern culture and social life.

2. Western/Modern culture is a fluid and loose term because it encompasses so many facets. Some central characteristics of Western/Modern culture include the following:

    a) Democracy

    b) Rational thinking

    c) Individualism

    d) Christianity

    e) Capitalism

    f) Modern technology

    g) Human rights

    h) Scientific thinking

3. It is agreed by most historians that the Ancient Greeks are responsible for the concept of the Western/ Modern culture.

    a) The Greeks were the first to build what has come to

be called Western/Modern civilization. Democracy along with critical advances in science, philosophy, and architecture are also attributed to the Greeks.

b) The Greeks and Romans pretty much founded Western/Modern culture and transmitted it to Europe, and from there it was transmitted to the Western Hemisphere.

III. **The Shift in Culture**

Though people affirm that a change has occurred in our culture and society, most do not understand how far culture has shifted. The America that I grew up in, a modern society still influenced by the church, is now a postmodern and strongly secular humanistic society; in fact, some even argue we are now in a post-postmodern culture.

A. Postmodernity

What is postmodernity or postmodern? Postmoderns do not place their philosophy into a defined box; however, the following characteristics appear to be elemental:

1. There is no absolute truth.[414] Postmoderns look at truth as a contrived illusion, misused to gain power over others.

2. Truth and error are synonymous. Facts are too limiting to determine anything. What is fact today can be error tomorrow.[415]

3. Self-conceptualization and rationalization[416] replace traditional logic and objectivity. Postmoderns reject the scientific method of determining facts and rely on opinions.

4. Traditional authority is false and corrupt.[417] Postmoderns speak against the constraints that religion places on morals and secular authority. They conduct an intellectual revolution against traditional establishment.

5. The fair way to administer goods and services is through collective ownership.

6. Modernism has produced disillusionment. Postmoderns feel remorse and regret over the unfulfilled promises of religion, science, technology, and government.

7. Morality is personal.[418] Postmoderns believe ethics to be relative and subject morality to personal opinion. Without the need to follow traditional values and rules, postmoderns define morality as each person's own code of ethics.

8. Globalization supersedes nationalism. National boundaries are a hindrance to human communications,[419] and nationalism leads to war.

9. All religions are valid.[420] Postmoderns value inclusive faiths and gravitate toward New Age religion, thus denouncing the Bible's exclusive claim that Jesus Christ is the only way to God.

10. Liberal ethics should prevail. Postmoderns defend the cause of homosexuals and feminists.[421]

11. Pro-environmentalism dictates behavior. Western society is to blame for the destruction of "Mother Earth," according to a postmodern.[422]

Basically, the postmodern philosophy is largely a reaction against the values, beliefs, philosophical assumptions, and the constructs of Enlightenment that modernity held. The postmoderns deny this Enlightenment and espouse faith in technology and science as instruments of human progress and yet postmoderns blame the development of technologies for the killing that occurred during the World Wars on such a massive scale.[423]

The American culture continues to be saturated with this philosoph-ical idea, propagated at different levels of society. Every corner of the country bears the mark of postmodernity's influence. Ross Parsley calls this the cultural tidal wave.[424]

B. Secular Humanism

Secular humanism touches every aspect of life including values, meaning, and identity, it is comprehensive. Secular humanism is broader than atheism, which concerns only the nonexistence of god or the supernatural. Important as that may be, there's a lot more to life ... and secular humanism addresses it.[425]

1. Secular humanism is referred to as *nonreligious,* espous-ing no belief in a realm or beings imagined to tran-scend ordinary experience.[426] From *Webster's Dictionary:*

    a) *Secular. "Pertaining to the world or things not spiritual or sacred."*

    b) *Humanism. "Any system of thought or action concerned with the interests or ideals of people ... the intellectual and cultural movement ... characterized by an emphasis on human interests rather than ... religion."* [427]

2. However, the word "religion" is defined in *Merriam-Webster Dictionary* as, "a cause, principle, or system of beliefs held to with ardor and faith."[428]

3. Secular humanism *is a lifestance,* or what Council for Secular Humanism founder Paul Kurtz has termed a *eupraxsophy*: a body of principles suitable for orienting a complete human life.[429]

    a) Eupraxsophy is any philosophy or life stand that does not rely on belief in the transcendent or supernatural.

    b) As a *secular* lifestance, secular humanism incorpor-ates the Enlightenment principle of *individualism*, which celebrates emancipating the individual from traditional controls by family, church, and state, increasingly empowering each of us to set the terms of his or her own life.[430]

4. Secular humanism is philosophically *naturalistic*. It holds that nature is all there is, and that reliable knowledge is best obtained when we inquiry nature using the scientific method. Naturalism declares that supernatural entities like God do not exist and goes on to say that knowledge gained without appeal to the natural world and without impartial review by multiple observers is unreliable.[431]

5. Secular humanism provides a *cosmic outlook*—a worldview in the broadest sense, grounding humanity in the context of our universe and relying on methods demonstrated by science. Secular humanists see themselves as undesigned, unintended beings who arose through evolution, possessing unique attributes of self-awareness and moral agency.[432]

6. Secular humanists hold that ethics is *consequential*, to be judged by results. This is in contrast to so-called command ethics, in which right and wrong are defined in advance and attributed to divine authority. "No god will save us," declared *Humanist Manifesto II* (1973), "we must save ourselves."[433] Secular humanists seek to develop and improve their ethical principles by examining the results they yield in the lives of real men and women.[434]

7. Secular Humanism is a worldview. That is, it is a set of beliefs through which one interprets all of reality. Second, Secular Humanism is a religious worldview. Do not let the word "secular" mislead you. The Humanists themselves would agree that they adhere to a religious worldview. According to the Humanist Manifestos I & II: Humanism is "a philosophical, religious, and moral point of view."[435]

8. Not all humanists, though, want to be identified as "religious," because they understand that religion is (supposedly) not allowed in American public education. To identify Secular Humanism as a religion

would eliminate the Humanists' main vehicle for the propagation of their faith. And it is a faith, by their own admission; according to The Humanist Mani-festos.[436]

9. Humanist Paul Kurtz, says that, "Humanism cannot in any fair sense of the word apply to one who still believes in God as the source and creator of the universe."[437]

10. Atheism leads most Secular Humanists to adopt ethical relativism—the belief that no absolute moral code exists, and therefore man must adjust his ethical standards in each situation according to his own judgment. If God does not exist, then He cannot establish an absolute moral code. Humanist Max Hocutt says that human beings "may, and do, make up their own rules... Morality is not discovered; it is made."[438]

Secular humanism can be defined as a religious worldview based on atheism, naturalism, evolution, and ethical relativism. But this definition is merely the tip of the iceberg.[439]

Fourth Session

"Joshua son of Nun, the servant of the LORD, died at the age of a hundred and ten. And they buried him in the land of his inheritance, at Timnath Heres in the hill country of Ephraim, north of Mount Gaash. After that whole **generation** had been gathered to their fathers, another **generation** grew up, who knew neither the LORD nor what he had done for Israel" (Judg 2:8-10, *emphasis added*).

I. **How Culture Has Affected the Generations**
Culture affects every part of life.

A. Culture is the unwritten code or rules of behavior. Everyone lives in culture, and no one can separate from the effects of culture. It is part of us, and we are part of it. Most people are not fully aware of culture's influence on their lives.

1. We use culture to order our lives, interpret our experiences, validate our beliefs, and evaluate everyone's

behavior; that means a person assesses not just their own behavior but also everyone else's around them.

    2. Culture is our resource for understanding experiences and helps to make sense of our own lives and the world around us.

B. What makes this so difficult to understand is that this is largely a mental reflex, an unconscious process, and that a person is hardly aware that it is taking place at all. What this means is people are being influenced by culture, and they really are not aware that it is affecting them.

C. This leads to the question of what your position or worldview is.

    1. This is dealing with your belief system, what governs your life, behavior, attitude, and lifestyle, everything. Are you

        a) Conservative _____

        b) Secular   _____

        c) Religious _____

        d) Modern   _____

        e) Humanistic _____

        f) Biblical   _____

        g) Evolutionary _____

        h) Postmodern _____

D. The truth is most people may claim to be one, but generally people have a mixture of a little from a couple of these different views.

II. **Worldview**

A recent nationwide survey completed by the Barna Research Group determined that only four percent of Americans had a "biblical" worldview.[440] When George Barna, who has researched cultural trends and the Christian Church since 1984, looked at the "born-again" believers in America, the results were "just one out of every ten."[441]

A. Barna's survey also connected an individual's worldview with his or her moral beliefs and actions.

1. Barna's recent research reveals that, although most people own a Bible and know some of its content, their research found that most Americans, five percent, are Bible centered.[442] Meaning most Americans have little idea how to integrate core biblical principles to form a unified and meaningful response to the challenges and opportunities of life.

B. **What is a worldview?**

1. A worldview is the framework from which we view reality and make sense of life and the world. "[It's] any ideology, philosophy, theology, movement, or religion that provides an overarching approach to understand-ing God, the world and man's relations to God and the world," says David Noebel, author of *Understanding the Times*.[443]

2. For example, a two-year old believes he's the center of his world, a secular humanist believes that the material world is all that exists, and a Buddhist believes he can be liberated from suffering by self-purification.[444]

3. "Someone with a biblical worldview believes his primary reason for existence is to love and serve God."[445]

C. Whether conscious or subconscious, every person has some type of worldview.[446]

1. "A personal worldview is a combination of all you believe to be true, and what you believe becomes the driving force behind every emotion, decision, and action."[447]

2. "Therefore, it affects your response to every area of life: from philosophy to science, theology and anthropology, to economics, law, politics, art and social order—everything."[448]

3. For example, let's suppose you have bought the idea that beauty is in the eye of the beholder (secular relative truth) as opposed to beauty as defined by God's purity and creativity (absolute truth). Then any art piece, no matter how vulgar or abstract, would be considered "art," a creation of beauty.[449]

D. What is your worldview?

1. This is dealing with your belief system, what governs your life, behavior, attitude, and lifestyle, everything. Are you

   a) Conservative _____

   b) Secular _____

   c) Religious _____

   d) Modern _____

   e) Humanistic _____

   f) Biblical _____

   g) Evolutionary _____

   h) Postmodern _____

E. As I mentioned, most people may claim to one but have a mixture of a little from a couple of these different views. What is your mix?

F. **What is a biblical worldview?**

1. "A biblical worldview is based on the infallible Word of God. When you believe the Bible is entirely true, then you allow it to be the foundation of everything you say and do."[450]

2. A biblical worldview is more than a religious belief system. It is, in fact, a complete and integrated frame-work through which to see the entire world.

3. A biblical worldview is a comprehensive view of the world from a biblical standpoint. This mean, a biblical worldview

Facilitator's Guide

should be an integrated whole, comprised of a number of distinct, biblical elements. In other words, each believer should filter his or her day through a pair of biblical/spiritual goggles and see the world as a harmonious set of beliefs and perspectives.

4. Here are areas on which a biblical worldview touches:

   a) Theology – Theism (Trinitarian);

   b) Philosophy – Supernaturalism (Faith and Reason);

   c) Ethics – Moral Absolutes;

   d) Science – Creationism;

   e) Psychology – Mind/Body (Fallen Nature of Man);

   f) Sociology – Traditional Family, Church, and State;

   g) Law – Divine/Natural Law;

   h) Politics – Justice, Freedom, and Order;

   i) Economics – Stewards of Property;

   j) History – Creation, Fall, and Redemption.

G. Do you have a biblical worldview?

1. Answer the following questions:

   a) Do absolute moral truths exist?

   b) Does the Bible define absolute truth?

   c) Did Jesus Christ live a sinless life?

   d) Is God the all-powerful and all-knowing Creator of the universe, and does He still rule it today?

   e) Is salvation a gift from God that cannot be earned?

   f) Is Satan real?

   g) Does a Christian have a responsibility to share his or her faith in Christ with other people?

h) Is the Bible accurate in all of its teachings?[451]

2. How many did you answer no to? _____

3. Did you answer yes to these? _____

   a) Only nine percent of "born-again" believers did.[452]

   b) But what's more important than your yes to these questions is whether your life shows it.[453]

   c) Granted, we are all sinners and fall short, but most of our gut reactions will reflect what we deep-down, honest-to-goodness believe to be real and true.[454]

III. How does a biblical worldview get diluted?

Here is the problem; we are bombarded with nonbiblical worldviews constantly from all avenues of the media, museums, books, and academia. So, dilution is possible if we do not keep ourselves in the Word of God. [455]

A. Another way dilution occurs is that we live in a selfish, fallen world, and these ideas seductively appeal to our sinful nature. Without realizing it, if we are not careful, we could end up incorporating anti-biblical ideas into our personal worldview.[456]

B. The seduction is very subtle. Our secular humanistic society is corrupting.

C. There are phrases in the Bible that state this world is corrupted (1 Pet 1:4; 2:20).

IV. Why does a biblical worldview matter?

If we do not really believe the truth of God and live it, then our witness will be confusing and misleading[457] (Heb 11:3).

A. Most go through life not recognizing that their personal worldviews have been deeply affected by the world.[458]

   1. "The secularized American view of history, law, politics, science, God and man affects our thinking more than we realize."[459]

2. Then we are taken "captive through hollow and deceptive philosophy, which depends on human tradition and the basic principles of this world rather than on Christ" (Col 2:8).

B. However, by diligently learning, applying, and trusting God's truths in every area of our lives, "we can begin to develop a deep comprehensive faith that will stand against the unrelenting tide of our culture's nonbiblical ideas."[460]

C. "Do not conform any longer to the pattern of this world, but be transformed by the renewing of your mind" (Rom 12:2). From the Message Bible, "Don't become so well-adjusted to your culture that you fit into it without even thinking. Instead, fix your attention on God" (Rom 12:2, MSG).[461]

- What stood out to you as being something new that you did not know before, with regard to culture, worldview, and biblical worldview?

- Have you ever thought about the influence of culture in your life? Upon your family?

- From this session, are there one or two ideas that you feel are critical to understand that would help your biblical/spiritual worldview?

Fifth Session

"For by him all things were created: things in heaven and on earth, visible and invisible, whether thrones or powers or rulers or authorities; all things were created by him and for him" (Col 1:16).

In this session, we are going to look at the biblical theological view of God designed for humanity. We will also look over the Fall and its consequences, God's intervention, and part I of God's cultural project.

I. **The Original Design**

From the beginning of Creation, the Lord intended humanity

to develop and live in culture. God set the foundation, laying the groundwork from the start when He "planted a garden in the east, in Eden; and there he put the man he had formed" (Gen 2:8).

A. It was the Lord God who established the beliefs, the parameters that humanity would live in, the directives for living together, and set the goals for humanity (Gen 1:26-28; 2:15-18, 23-25).

B. The biblical story begins revealing a God who is not hidden (Gen 1:1-2; 2:7, 19; 3:8).

1. Of all that God created, it is only when humans are created that the Bible provides more specific details, emphasizing humanity's importance. To further stress humanity's standing in creation, God spoke to Himself to create man, male and female, in His own image. He did not say for the land or soil to create humankind.[462] "Then God said, 'Let us make man in our image, in our likeness...'" (Gen 1:26).

2. Though man was the pinnacle of God's creation, the importance placed on the Garden is seen only after man is placed there. "The LORD God took the man and put him in the Garden of Eden to work it and take care of it" (Gen 2:15).[463]

3. The very words "to work it and take care of it" stress the value of importance God placed on the Garden and its contents. This man and woman find themselves, as all humans find themselves, in the midst of an unfolding story.[464]

C. The Beginning of God's Culture Project

1. The first three chapters of Genesis provide insight into this God who is Creator. This human, created in God's own image, will be someone with whom God will commune and in whom He will delight. In addition, this human will know the pleasure of God's presence, love, and favor through living in fellowship with Him.

It was intended for humanity to live dependent on this Creator for life and existence in this world.[465]

2. The Lord is the first gardener, and the One who originated the first culture.[466] "Now the LORD God had planted a garden in the east, in Eden; and there he put the man he had formed" (Gen 2:8).

   a) Somewhere between the third day of creating plant life and the sixth day, the Lord God planted a beautiful garden specially prepared for Adam.[467]

   b) When Adam was placed in the Garden, the Lord also established a set of values and beliefs when boundaries were established so Adam could enjoy the Garden and avoid failure.[468] "You are free to eat from any tree in the garden but you must not eat from the tree of the knowledge of good and evil, for when you eat of it you will surely die" (Gen 2:16-17).

3. Culture is what humanity makes of the world in which they live.[469] "The LORD God took the man and put him in the Garden of Eden to work it and take care of it" (Gen 2:15).

   a) Adam had been given certain directives regarding this Garden. He was told to cultivate, to tend, and care for this Garden. These directives were added to the delegated authority already spoken over mankind to fulfill.[470] "God blessed them and said to them, 'Be fruitful and increase in number; fill the earth and subdue it. Rule over the fish of the sea and the birds of the air and over every living creature that moves on the ground'" (Gen 1:28).

   b) The care and tending to creation are humanity's mission.[471] Adam was made a responsible being to share in taking care of God's creation. It was never intended for the gifts God gave to be neglected, misused, or wasted. Since God is active, people should be active serving Him wherever the Lord places them.

4. A Counterculture Begun

   a) Adam and Eve failed in keeping the culture God established for them resulting in a counterculture being created that now runs against the values and beliefs of the Lord.

   b) Genesis 3 records the dialogue between Eve and the serpent. Eve's encounter with the serpent reveals the cultural values and beliefs by which Adam and Eve lived. "The woman said to the serpent, 'We may eat fruit from the trees in the garden,' but God did say, 'You must not eat fruit from the tree that is in the middle of the garden, and you must not touch it, or you will die'" (Gen 3:2-3).

   c) From any tree in the Garden the humans could eat except one. "Culture is the realm of human freedom" containing in this freedom the "constraints and impossibilities," which are "the boundaries within."[472]

   d) The serpent's question, "Did God really say, 'You must not eat from any tree in the garden'?" (Gen 3:1) really denied the love of God and intended to suggest, "How could God keep any good thing from you if He loves you?"

   e) The serpent's purpose intended to draw attention away from all the good God had given them and to focus Eve and Adam's attention on the one thing they could not have.[473]

   f) How did the serpent achieve his goal? He assisted Eve in changing her values and beliefs about the fruit that was forbidden by raising doubts in the accountability of God's Word, in His purpose for mankind,[474] and in the parameters that God had set.

   1) Eve's perspective was altered; she originally

saw the fruit as detestable and dangerous to the touch, but now she "saw that the fruit of the tree was good for food and pleasing to the eye, and also desirable for gaining wisdom" (Gen 3:6).

2) The temptation was far more diabolical than humanity thought. The serpent twisted and degraded the divine image that humanity received by craftily and deceitfully describing it as being like God, knowing good and evil (Gen 3:5).[475]

3) Instead of being a cultivator with God, humanity now is a consumer,[476] "she took some and ate it. She also gave some to her husband ... and he ate it" (Gen 3:6).

g) Adam and Eve were not forced to eat what was forbidden; the serpent only helped to change their values and beliefs. With craftiness, the devil was able to corrupt the culture God was creating with the choice Adam and Eve made. "And the LORD God commanded the man, 'You are free to eat from any tree in the garden; but you must not eat from the tree of the knowledge of good and evil, for when you eat of it you will surely die" (Gen 2:16-17).

1) Eating from that one tree, the tree of the knowledge of good and evil, Adam and Eve died spiritually. Death in the Bible primarily means separation.[477]

h) Now, through disobedience Adam and Eve broke fellowship with God. Since humans are both spiritual and physical beings, following Adam and Eve's disobedience, they died spiritually and are now at odds with God.

1) The immediate effects resulted in humankind experiencing guilt, shame, rejection, weakness, and helplessness.[478] Instantly, their eyes were

opened and now they had knowledge of good and evil but through their own experience.

2) Instead of them being like God, Adam and Eve are now filled with shame, realizing they are naked.

3) This cultural community in which God intended for humanity to experience His presence and work to cultivate and nurture this good creation is now marred with disobedience and rebellion.[479] Humanity now inherits a value system that is flawed and blemished.[480]

5. Broken Promises

   a) The serpent produced an illusion, and the promises of wisdom and godlikeness were a deception and lie. Adam and Eve exchanged their enjoyment of God's fellowship for separation and exile from His kingdom.[481]

      1) Now their nakedness caused them to be aware; they had nothing to hide their guilt.[482] Their very first act after their consumption of the fruit and loss of fellowship with God was to make fig leaves into some type of clothing.

      2) Instead of Adam and Eve enjoying the good Garden planted for them with a good God and His presence, they are now trying to pro-tect themselves from the broken fellowship with this good God and from one another.[483]

   b) The devil was able to warp the culture God had intended, and now a new set of values and beliefs would direct the future cultures of the world. From the sewing of fig leaves onward, culture would be intertwined with sin.[484]

      1) From Genesis 3 through 11, culture is spiraling downward as sin ravishes humanity. As

humanity increases in numbers, with every new generation, cultures rise and fall.[485]

2) The counterculture that began with a choice in the Garden of Eden is now considered normal, and that culture is ever-changing, increasing its values and beliefs that are more anti-God.[486]

3) The culture God intended to establish is considered the counterculture to humanity's progressiveness. Humanity's alienation from God and one another only descends into greater shame, filled with violence and perversion of culture.[487]

6. God's Intervention

Again, I want to emphasize that culture is the accumulation of experiences, beliefs, values, attitudes, hierarchies, roles, concepts, and systems of knowledge shared by a group of people. Culture began with God, though that culture has been perverted and distorted. Neither God nor His standards and commandments are in anyway corrupted; it is through humanity's choices that culture is corrupted.

a) Due to Adam and Eve's decision to rebel against God's command, the will of humankind is also affected so that each person is now faced with multiple choices each day.[488] Adam and Eve only had one bad choice to make in the Garden. Now, humankind is faced with a myriad of good and bad choices every day.

b) With the whole world fallen, God had a plan to intervene in order to see a culture developed that would be a testimony of His grace. This cultural project was to be established around a set of standards that would direct humanity's decisions for living in a healthy relationship with God and one another.[489]

c) This is exemplified as God intervenes in Israel's history, first in choosing and calling a man named Abram (Gen 12:1). Abram, known better as Abraham, the father of the Jewish people and eventually the father of all people, chose to live a life of faith in God; "he is the father of all who believe" (Rom 4:11).[490]

   1) God singles out Abram for this distinct pur-pose: to make of him a great nation (Gen 12:2). Just as the Lord God provided a more permanent covering for Adam and Eve, animal skins for fig leaves, God now chooses culture to show His mercy on a vastly grander and longer scale.[491] Through the family of Abram, the Lord God chooses to demon-strate to the rest of the world filled with multiple and conflicting cultures how a nation depends for its identity, security, and very existence of God.[492]

   2) A believer's hope for growth, meaning, and fulfillment is tied to the understanding of their identity. Understanding who God is and a person's relationship to Him is the foundation of an individual's belief system and behavior patterns as a Christian.[493]

   3) When the Lord changed Abram's name to Abraham (Gen 17:5), God's agenda was to create something new, something that had not existed before, a nation that belonged to Him in a special way.[494]

II. **Reinstituting God's Cultural Project Part I**

This cultural project would unfold through Abraham and Sarah's son Isaac, then through Isaac and Rebekah's son Jacob. This cultural project continued through the twelve children of Jacob and his wives Leah, Rachel, Bilhah, and Zilpah, and all their descendants. As this project unfolded, Abraham's descendants relocated to a foreign country where their population multiplied, but they eventually found themselves in bondage to the indigenous people of Egypt.

A. The Lord foretold this to Abraham shortly after his call.[495] "Then the LORD said to him, 'Know for certain that your descendants will be strangers in a country not their own, and they will be enslaved and mistreated four hundred years'" (Gen 15:13).

1. Abraham's descendants moved to Egypt due to a severe famine that plagued the known world (Gen 41:56-57). Initially, Pharaoh and the people of Egypt showed hospitality, kindness, and extended favor to Abraham's descendants. However, as time passed, a new Pharaoh arose, unfamiliar with the reason the Israelites were living in Egypt.

2. This new Pharaoh led his people in fear to act hostilely toward Abraham's descendants—the Israelites.

    a) "Look," he [Pharoah] said to his people, "the Israelites have become much too numerous for us. Come, we must deal shrewdly with them or they will become even more numerous and, if war breaks out, will join our enemies, fight against us and leave the country." So they put slave masters over them to oppress them with forced labor, and they built Pithom and Rameses as store cities for Pharaoh (Exod 1:9-11).

3. This may not sound like the beginning of a great cultural project, but it sets the stage for God to emerge as one who is concerned for humanity's sorrowful condition.

4. God emerges on the scene as the Redeemer by revealing Himself to a man named Moses.

    a) Moses's supernatural encounter in Exodus 3 sets the juncture for God to start forming the foundation for His cultural project. Starting a new culture rests more in what God wanted the Israelites to be; that is, seeing with eyes of faith what God was expecting them to become and then striving to embody those values.[496]

B. The Cultural Goal

1. Before moving further into the values of culture, it is important to describe the Lord's goal for this new cultural project.

2. The revelation of God's objective occurred at the base of the mountain of God (Exod 3:12) where Moses received his commissioning.

   a) "And God said, 'I will be with you. And this will be the sign to you that it is I who have sent you: When you have brought the people out of Egypt, you will worship God on this mountain.'"

   b) The sign that the Lord was literally with Moses would be success in delivering the Israelites from bondage and when Moses brought the people to the Lord at that very mountain so they could worship Him.

3. In chapter 19, another glimpse of God's cultural goal is expressed. The Lord instructs Moses to share with the people:

   "Then Moses went up to God, and the LORD called to him from the mountain and said, 'This is what you are to say to the house of Jacob and what you are to tell the people of Israel: 'You yourselves have seen what I did to Egypt, and how I carried you on eagles' wings and brought you to myself. Now if you obey me fully and keep my covenant, then out of all nations you will be my treasured possession. Although the whole earth is mine, you will be for me a kingdom of priests and a holy nation.' These are the words you are to speak to the Israelites" (Exod 19:3-6).

4. Again, the Lord stresses that He was the one who delivered the nation of Israel from bondage and brought them to himself.

5. The cultural goal is to make the nation of Israel His own treasured possession, for the people to accept their identity as a kingdom of priests, and for Israel to collectively grow into a holy nation.

6. Interestingly, this very idea is not only found here in Exodus 19 but in the New Testament as well. In the book of 1 Peter, one of the original twelve apostles declared,

   a) "But you are a chosen people, a royal priesthood, a holy nation, a people belonging to God, that you may declare the praises of him who called you out of darkness into his wonderful light" (1 Pet 2:9).

   b) John, also one of the original apostles, was banished on the Island of Patmos as a prisoner for faithfully preaching about Jesus and the Word of God. While John lived banished there, he received the final word or vision from the Lord recorded in the book of Revelation.[497]

   c) As John initially encounters Jesus, he receives this revelation of Jesus Christ and writes,

   "To him who loves us and has freed us from our sins by his blood, and has made us to be a kingdom and priests to serve his God and Father—to him be glory and power for ever and ever! Amen" (Rev 1:5-6).

7. The cultural goal of the Lord for His people Israel and for the Church was to become a treasured possession, a holy nation, and a royal priesthood.

C. Cultural Values

This cultural project begins with God; He is the founda-tion stone or the "chief cornerstone" (Matt 21:24).

1. The Lord God initiated the contact with Moses; Moses did not seek God for help to deliver his people from bondage.

2. Just like the beginning of creation, God created the

universe and the world in which humanity lives. God created humanity, planted a garden in Eden, and placed Adam and Eve there.

    a) The Lord gave the parameters for humankind to live and act in Eden. Once Adam and Eve sinned, it was God who came looking for them since they broke fellowship with Him. And it was God who provided a more lasting covering by slaying the first animal, trading humankind's fig leaf clothing for something a little more permanent, leather skins.

3. Centuries have passed, and now God is calling Moses for He has heard and seen Israel's hardships. Moses was not seeking the Lord but serving as a shepherd, tending the flock of his father-in-law, hiding still from Egypt (Exod 3:1).[498]

    a) However, that would not stop the Lord from seeking Moses. The Lord God uses a burning bush that is not consumed; He uses a supernatural manifestation to attract Moses.

    b) It is when Moses turns to look at this strange phenomenon that the Lord speaks to him. As Moses draws close, the Lord calls from the midst of the flame to him.

    c) God knew Moses's location and his name; He knew the exact moment that Moses would pass that spot of the burning bush, and the desperate plight of the Israelites.

        1) The LORD said, "I have indeed seen the misery of my people in Egypt. I have heard them crying out because of their slave drivers, and I am concerned about their suffering. So I have come down to rescue them from the hand of the Egyptians and to bring them up out of that land into a good and spacious land, a land flowing with milk and honey—the home of

the Canaanites, Hittites, Amorites, Perizzites, Hivites and Jebusites. And now the cry of the Israelites has reached me, and I have seen the way the Egyptians are oppressing them" (Exod 3:7-9).

d) These verses provide revelation of the attributes and decrees of God in His calling Moses.[499] He sees, hears, and is concerned about the harsh suffering of the people of Israel.

e) In Exodus chapter 2, God expresses His concern, "God heard their groaning and he remembered his covenant with Abraham, with Isaac and with Jacob" (Exod 2:24).

   1) God heard the people's groaning and remembered the covenant He made with Abraham. Verse 25 tells readers that "God looked on the Israelites" and was concerned (Exod 2:25).

f) The Lord God uses this burning bush experience to reveal something about His own character and glory to Moses. God reveals "the glory of His unchanging, mediated salvation which remains the hope and encouragement of those who are in slavery and bondage."[500]

g) As Moses turns to investigate this strange manifestation, immediately God identifies one of His moral attributes, holiness.[501] The Lord began to teach Moses about His holiness by not allowing him to proceed too far on His holiness.[502]

   1) The Lord accomplishes this by giving Moses a simple instruction to follow, the ground he was stepping onto was holy, and Moses was required to remove his sandals.

   2) The ground did not become holy due to Moses stepping onto that sacred soil; God's presence

made it holy (Exod 3:1-5).[503] Once his shoes were removed, Moses stopped proceeding closer, and hiding his face, he heard God identify himself, "I am the God of your father, the God of Abraham, the God of Isaac and the God of Jacob" (Exod 3:6).

3) Referencing the Patriarchs shows Moses that this is not a new or unknown God but One who made a covenant with the fathers of the nation Israel and who remembers His promise to them.[504] God's covenant-relation to His people is humanity's best support and greatest encouragement to faith.[505]

4) This God is moved by compassion for suffer-ing people, and then He declares a plan of rescue.

h) Though this story includes Moses's call and commissioning, it really is about God's concern, compassion, and covenant with a man named Abraham. "I will make you into a great nation and ... all peoples on earth will be blessed through you" (Gen 12:2-3).

1) Once again, just as the Lord God had created culture in the Garden of Eden, He is about to start this cultural project with slaves, a culture that was to be defined by faith.[506]

i) It is interesting that the Lord announced He would come down to rescue the Israelites from their misery and distress; however, Moses is assigned the responsibility to accomplish that task (Exod 3:9-10).

j) The Lord had chosen Moses, an eighty-year-old fugitive running from Egyptian justice, to accomplish the impossible task "of leading 2.5 million crushed and hopeless slaves out of the control of the mightiest empire on earth."[507]

1) Moses's response to the mission possibly resonates with many a leader feeling the enormity of the call and responsibility to ministry, "Who am I?" (Exod 3:11).

2) The Lord met Moses's sense of inadequacy with the promise of His presence and the assurance of success (Exod 3:12). The theme of God's presence is one of the major subjects in Exodus.[508]

3) Moses's insecurities and inadequacies are met with the full and complete adequacy of God's presence. The Lord felt that His presence was enough to meet any challenge Moses would face.[509]

k) The importance of God's presence as a cultural value is stressed when Israel sins by worshipping the golden calf (Exod 32:7-8).

1) God removes His presence and promises an alternative (Exod 33:2-3). The value of the presence of God was so important to the culture that Moses asked the Lord not to move the nation of Israel without promising to go with them (Exod 33:15).

l) The people had forfeited God's favorable pre-sence through their disobedience of worshipping the golden calf.[510] Moses understood the impor-tance of this loss so he pleads with God to restore His presence, for it was the mark that was to distinguish the people of God from those who were not God's people (Exod 33:12-16).

1) This, above all, was the unique characteristic of this cultural project, God's presence among His people. This stresses the importance that the people of God are to be presence driven more than program or purpose driven; "those who

are led by the Spirit of God are sons of God" (Rom 8:14; Gal 5:16).[511]

2) Also, this was one of the main building blocks for this cultural project, a presence driven culture.[512]

m) Returning to the unfolding dialogue between Moses and the Lord, the Lord responds to Moses's objection to go to Egypt with the promise of His abiding presence and guidance,[513] which should have been enough for Moses.[514]

1) God's promise contained two elements: first, was God's assurance that He would go with Moses and provide direction. Second, God promised success.[515]

2) The Lord provided a sign of success or fulfillment for Moses: "When you have brought the people out of Egypt, you will worship God on this mountain" (Exod 3:12).

3) God's purpose for this deliverance was so the children of Israel could worship Him at the mountain of God. This is stressed frequently in the book of Exodus (Exod 4:23; 7:16; 8:1, 20; 9:1, 13; 10:3, 7-8, 11, 24, 26; 12:31).[516]

4) The Hebrew word "worship" is the same word for "serve" or "to be a slave."[517] Israel was serving as slaves to the Egyptians; but after the Lord delivered them and brought the Israelites to the mountain of God, they would serve and worship Him as His subjects.[518]

- Dealing with culture, have you ever heard before that God intended for culture to be part of His purpose for humanity?

- From this session, what stood out to you as being important for culture?

In Moses's calling, is there something unique about this encounter that you never considered?

Sixth Session

"For the creation waits with eager longing for the revealing of the sons of God. For the creation was subjected to futility, not willingly, but because of him who subjected it, in hope that the creation itself will be set free from its bondage to corruption and obtain the freedom of the glory of the children of God" (Rom 8:19-21, ESV).[519]

From the beginning of Creation, the Lord intended humanity to develop and live in culture. God set the foundation, laying the groundwork from the start when He "planted a garden in the east, in Eden; and there he put the man he had formed" (Gen 2:8). It was the Lord God who established the beliefs, the parameters that humanity would live in, the directives for living together, and the goals for humanity (Gen 1:26-28; 2:15-18, 23-25).

However, humanity chose to believe an illusion, a promise that was a ruse, which did not and could not fulfill what the serpent suggested. Yet, what God promised did come to pass, humankind died in their fellowship and relationship with God. Spiritual death occurred immediately, with physical death following in time. The culture God intended had been corrupted, and now humanity is subject to live life intertwined with sin.

But God had a plan, a cultural project.

I. Reinstituting God's Cultural Project Part II

This cultural project begins with God; He is the foundation stone or the "chief cornerstone" (Matt 21:24).

   A. Cultural Values, continued

   1. One final value or foundational stone to be discussed here in the initiation for this cultural project is God's name.

      a) Moses questioned the Lord on what name was he to provide to the elders of Israel if they were to ask for it. The Lord God provided, "I AM WHO I AM" (Exod 3:14).

      b) In the past, those who knew the Lord before Moses's encounter on the mountain of God knew God as *El* or *Elohim*, as *El-Elyon*—that is, the Most High. They also knew Him as Shaddai—that is the Almighty, but as early as the time of Seth, they knew the Lord as *Yahweh*, but it had been lost.[520]

      c) *Yahweh* is the name that God chose, for it is His only personal Name; all the rest are titles. This revelation is being renewed with God officially calling Moses and giving His personal name.[521]

B. Also, in connection with this final value is God calling Moses by his name. From the burning bush, God addresses Moses personally. By saying, "Moses! Moses!", God was using a form called "repetition of endearment. In ancient Semitic culture, addressing someone by saying his or her name twice was a way of expressing endearment, that is, affection and friendship."[522]

   1. This is amplified not only by the fact of the Lord expressing His endearment and friendship to Moses by calling his name twice, but also by the Lord giving Moses His personal name, *Yahweh*.

C. Here are the foundational stones or values for this new cultural project:

   1. God is personally interested in being a friend; the sharing of names (Exod 3:4, 14);

   2. This personal God cares about people, their bondages and struggles. He sees, hears, is concerned, and has a plan for rescue (Exod 3:7-9);

   3. This God is holy, and He expects to be respected as such (Exod 3:5);

4. He remembers the promises He has made. In other words, He is a covenant God who keeps His end of the covenant (Exod 3:6, 8);

5. God's purpose for rescuing people is that they willingly serve and worship Him (Exod 3:12).

D. One final stone or value to be woven into the very fabric of this new culture is the importance of the blood of the lamb. Even with all the judgments God passed on Pharaoh and Egypt, Pharaoh never gave up his opposition to the will and purpose of Jehovah until the Lamb was slain.[523] The Passover was the final plague that would cause Pharaoh to submit to God and release the Israelites from their bondage (Exod 11:1; 12:12-13).

E. Cultural Principles

1. With Egypt lying in ruins, wasted, and Pharaoh's power broken, Israel has been delivered. Leaping forward, Israel has arrived at the base of the mountain of God (Exod 19:2).

    a) God's agenda was to create something that had not yet existed: a nation, a group of people who belonged to Him in a special way. This cultural project would unfold over time, bearing a complex but rich testimony to the world that the Lord God loves.

    b) As Creator of heaven and earth, He wanted to be represented to the nations as One dwelling in the midst of Israel.[524] Here is an important principle regarding culture: it is not created instantly. It takes time to build, develop, and shift culture that reflects and responds to God's interventions.

2. As stated earlier under Cultural Goal, God desired to nurture Israel into becoming His treasured possession, a kingdom of priests (Exod 19:5-6). However, God placed a condition on Israel for this to happen. Israel

would have to fully obey and keep the covenant God would make with them.

    a) What God expected was more than some sort of national treaty between Him and Israel. This contract that God instituted at Sinai involved each Israelite believer, and He expected each one to commit to it.

    b) The Lord considered this "commitment as binding as the vows taken by bride and groom at a wedding ceremony. Their very hearts and wills were called for, not just a pledge of allegiance on the part of the group."[525]

    c) The Lord expected and required each person in the Nation of Israel to be completely faithful and obedient to the covenant He was about to reveal.[526]

3. What is unique regarding this first encounter Israel has at the mountain of God is this—the expectation of obedience.

    a) Moses received instructions from God, and he was to go tell the people what was expected of them. In obedience, Moses gathers the elders of the tribes of Israel setting "before them all the words the Lord had commanded him to speak" (Exod 19:7).

    b) The people responded in unison, "We will do everything the Lord has said" (Exod 19:8). All of this is happening before the Lord has given the first commandment, the first instruction on worship, or any other demand on the people.

    c) By faith, the people of Israel said yes to whatever God laid down for them to obey. In other words, from these words Israel "pledged themselves to make obedience to God the guiding principle of their lives."[527]

4. It was after this commitment from Israel that the Lord

stated He would descend unto Mount Sinai in a dark cloud with thunder and lightning.

a) Moses took the people out of the camp to the mountain so they could meet with God. At the base of the mountain Moses and the people waited as the whole mountain became engulfed with smoke as the Lord descended in fire.

b) The whole mountain trembled violently, and the Israelites heard the sound of a trumpet, which grew louder and louder. Then Moses called to the Lord, and He responded.

c) The people of Israel literally heard God speak to Moses calling him to come up the mountain (Exod 19:9, 14-20). Now the Lord God estab-lishes holiness with the nation of Israel (Exod 19:12-13, 21-22). Another principle that was being established in this new cultural project is God's holiness.

5. It is during this interview with the Lord God that Moses is called to ascend to the top of the mountain (Exod 19:20).

a) Though specific instructions were given to the people not to touch the mountain, God again gives a very specific directive, "The LORD said to him, 'Go down and warn the people so they do not force their way through to see the LORD and many of them perish'" (Exod 19:21).

b) This is very interesting; the Lord emphasizes again His parameters of holiness, and He wants Moses to remind the people of these parameters. However, God is setting the stage for Him to speak the Ten Commandments to the people.

6. In chapter 20, the very first verse "emphasizes that God spoke the Ten Words/Ten Commandments Himself directly to Israel rather than through the intermediation

of Moses."[528]

    a) The preamble and prologue appear in verse 2 identifying the parties involved in this covenant agreement. "I am the Lord your God who brought you out..." (Exod 20:2).

    b) In the preamble, Israel is the recipient, identified by the "you" and the "Lord God" identifies himself as the giver of the covenant. This distinguishes that this is a two-party covenant, connecting the Lord God and His people Israel in an official legal relationship. What is interesting is that the Lord uses the singular pronoun, "you" for the nation of Israel.

    c) This represents how the Lord views the nation of Israel, as a unit. It also connects to the agreement made in chapter 19, where the whole nation, every person as one unit, agreed to God's commands. The latter part of verse 2 is the prologue explain-ing how the parties came to be related. It states, "who brought you out of Egypt, out of the land of slavery" (Exod 20:2). Since the Lord had rescued Israel from slavery, He has a claim to the people.[529]

7. With Moses and the people at the base of the mountain, God speaks the Ten Commandments audibly to them. The Ten Commandments would become the guiding principles for this new cultural project. This is a short list from Exodus 20 of those principles:

    a) You shall have no other gods before Me.

    b) You shall not make idols.

    c) You shall not take the name of the LORD your God in vain.

    d) Remember the Sabbath day, to keep it holy.

    e) Honor your father and your mother.

f) You shall not murder.

g) You shall not commit adultery.

h) You shall not steal.

i) You shall not bear false witness against your neighbor.

j) You shall not covet.

8. Another core principle revealed in chapter 20 of Exodus is the fear of the Lord (Exod 20:20). Hearing God speak audibly, along with seeing Mount Sinai consumed in smoke, hearing the thunder, seeing the lightning, and hearing a trumpet blowing, the Israelites trembled in fear.

9. The Israelites misinterpreted this whole experience.

   a) The Israelites determined that they only wanted Moses to speak to them, for they concluded they would die if God continued to speak to them (Exod 20:18-19). It was a choice of convenience for the people.[530]

10. Moses made it very clear that God was testing them, for He wanted them to fear Him, but not to be afraid of Him (Exod 20:20).

    a) Instead of being in awe of God, the people shrank back in intimidation, retreating from God's presence. A further explanation of God's manifestation is that Moses reassured the people that God's closeness was a means of testing them to see if they really would be afraid of sinning and disobeying Him.[531]

11. Worship is also one of the main principles for this new cultural project. The Lord is providing Moses instructtions on worship that were to be communicated to the people (Exod 20:22-25).

12. A central key of the corporate worship that the Lord expects of the Israelites is revealed in the Lord's promise of divine guidance and protection. God said He was "sending an angel ahead of [them] along the way... to bring [them] to the place [He] prepared" (Exod 23:20). The importance here is the directives associated with worship. Though this is not always identified with worship, this passage provides some interesting pieces of worship. The parts of worship identified in Exodus 23:20-33 are the following:

   a) Attentiveness to what is spoken and do not rebel against the Angel (v. 21);

   b) If the people obeyed all that the Angel spoke, then the Lord would be an enemy to all who were Israel's enemies and to any who oppose them He would oppose (v. 22);

   c) Based on Israel's obedience, the Lord would go ahead and drive out all those who stood in the way of them possessing the land; the promise (v. 23);

   d) Israel is not to bow down to worship the enemies' idols or gods and Israel must demolish all their enemies' sacred items of worship (v. 24);

   e) If Israel fulfills the above directive and worships only the Lord God, then the Lord promises all of this:

      1) To bless their food and water;

      2) He will take sickness away from among them;

      3) No woman will miscarry or be barren;

      4) He will give a full life (vv. 25-26);

      5) The Lord will send terror ahead of the Israelites and throw their enemies into confu-sion, and make all of them turn and run (v. 27);

6) The Lord will send ahead of the Israelites the hornet to drive out all those who possess the land, the promise; but only a little at a time until Israel is strong enough and large enough in number to take full possession of the land (vv. 28-30);

7) Also, the Lord will expand the borders of the nation of Israel to its fullest extent promised (v. 31);

8) Again, the Lord promises to hand over all the people who live in the land of Canaan for the Israelites to drive them out (v. 31).

f) To finalize these promises, God warned the Israelites not to allow any of the foreign people to stay in the land. The Lord emphasizes the importance of this telling the Israelites exactly what would happen; those foreign people would cause them to sin against the Lord God by worshiping their gods (vv. 32-33).

g) The Lord stated that one of the foundational stones for this cultural project would be service and worship of Him (Exod 3:12). In addition to worship being one of the foundational stones, once Israel was at the base of Mount Sinai, the Lord expanded worship as a core principle, which included His holiness (Exod 19:12-13, 21-22).

II. A Cultural Responsibility

The cultural principles were established over the first few months of Israel's deliverance from Egypt as they camped at the base of the mountain of God.

A. The Lord went into great detail defining and explaining the principles this new cultural project would live by, which covered moral, civil, and ceremonial codes. Also, during the time Israel spent at the mountain of God, they literally experienced different manifestations of God's physical presence. In addition, Israel received the construction pattern for the Tabernacle, the instructions for the priest, along with the special garments to be fabricated for the priest, and how those garments were to be worn by the priest.

B. Moses made it known that God's choice of Israel was marked by grace.[532]

1. The LORD did not set his affection on you and choose you because you were more numerous than other peoples, for you were the fewest of all peoples. But it was because the LORD loved you and kept the oath he swore to your forefathers that he brought you out with a mighty hand and redeemed you from the land of slavery, from the power of Pharaoh king of Egypt. Know therefore that the LORD your God is God; he is the faithful God, keeping his covenant of love to a thousand generations of those who love him and keep his commands (Deut 7:7-9).

C. Returning to Moses's call in Exodus 3, a statement is made by the Lord God that is also part of the founda-tional stones not highlighted earlier.

1. "God also said to Moses, 'Say to the Israelites, The LORD, the God of your fathers—the God of Abraham, the God of Isaac and the God of Jacob—has sent me to you. This is my name forever, the name by which I am to be remembered from generation to generation'" (Exod 3:15).

D. Of course, verse 15 is following verse 14 where the Lord provided the name Moses would tell the elders. God shared His personal name, "I AM WHO I AM" (Exod 3:14).

1. *Yahweh* is the name God chose for the Israelites to know Him. *Yahweh* was His personal Name; all the rest of the names used for God are titles.[533] This personal name of God was to be passed on from generation to generation. From God's Word Translation the latter

Facilitator's Guide

part of verse 15 states, "This is my name forever. This is my title throughout every generation" (Exod 3:15, GW).[534] The personal name of the Lord, *Yahweh*, was to be communicated from one generation to the next.

E. Cultural Mentoring

1. It is not made exactly clear why or when Moses chose Joshua as his aide, but Joshua is introduced when the Israelites were traveling from Egypt to the mountain of God.

2. It is also interesting that Moses chose Joshua in preference to other leaders older than forty years of age. Presumably, Moses had found him to possess unusual gifts of courage and godliness, which is why when the Amalekites attacked the Israelites, Moses told Joshua,[535] "Choose some of our men and go out to fight the Amalekites" (Exod 17:9).

3. The number of troops Joshua led is not revealed, but it is clear that the group of resistant fighters who faced the Amalekite raiders won the battle due to God's help (Exod 17:10-14).

4. Something unique is provided here: God told Moses to record this victory on a scroll and be sure Joshua heard it.

   a) *The New Living Translation*, verse 14 states, "Write this down on a scroll as a permanent reminder, and read it aloud to Joshua" (Exod 17:14, NLT).[536]

   b) In addition to recording this victory and reciting it to Joshua, Moses built an altar and worshiped the Lord for Moses was being sure the Lord received credit for the victory.

   c) A new name of the Lord is introduced in this moment of worship, *Jehovahnissi*, or *Yahwehnissi*, which means, "the LORD is my banner" (Exod 17:15). Under His banner, in His name and strength, believers win the battles they face.[537]

5. In addition to being Moses's aid, it appears that when Moses, Aaron and his sons, along with the seventy elders were invited to ascend to a place on the mountain where they would see God, Joshua was included in that group.

   a) This group of men saw God on His throne with a pavement of sapphire under His feet; they saw His hands, for it is stated that God did not raise His hand against these elders (Exod 24:11).

6. In addition, these leaders drank and ate a meal before God. Apparently, food and drink were prepared by heaven for these leaders. The NLT states, "In fact, they ate a covenant meal, eating and drinking in his presence!" (Exod 24:11).

   a) *The Bible Knowledge Commentary* affirms this idea that the elders were ratifying the covenant with a meal.[538] Along with the elders, the people had just promised earlier to obey all that the Lord had spoken to them through Moses (Exod 24:3).

   b) Now, the seventy elders, Aaron and his sons, Moses, and Joshua are invited up to see God (Exod 24:9-11). An important point is this group of men was able to proceed up the mountain of God to see His presence due to a sacrifice that was offered and sprinkling of the blood on all the people (Exod 24:4-8).

7. Though Joshua is not mentioned in the invitation earlier, he must have been in the midst of all of this activity for it is here that he is identified as Moses's aide (Exod 24:13), and Joshua was the only one out of the seventy elders and Aaron and his sons to receive this invitation to accompany Moses further up the mountain of God.

8. Moses instructs the elders to wait for him and his assistant, Joshua, for they would return to them (Exod 24:14). There is no record that the Lord told Moses to bring his assistant with him, but there is no record that the Lord objected to Joshua accompanying Moses.

F. Moses saw certain qualities that encouraged him to choose Joshua. This relationship grew so that Moses led this younger person to accompany him to experience God's unique presence. Moses and Joshua traveled up the mountain to a specific location, and the glory of the Lord covered the mountain.

1. With Joshua at his side, Moses waited for six days in the glory until the Lord specifically called for Moses only to proceed further (Exod 24:15-16). This remarkable experience must have left an indelible mark on Joshua's soul, for a few chapters later when Moses attended to the Tent of the Lord, it is stated, "The LORD would speak to Moses face to face, as a man speaks with his friend. Then Moses would return to the camp, but his young aide, Joshua, son of Nun, did not leave the tent" (Exod 33:11).

2. Moses would proceed to the Tent of the Lord, the earlier version of the Tabernacle, and the cloud of God's presence would descend onto the Tent. On this particular occasion, Joshua is with Moses lingering at the door as Moses is conversing with the Lord.

3. Only Joshua, now forty years of age, shared in this personal fellowship and service. Moses's future successor was being personally discipled, mentored, and prepared for his future position as leader.

G. At the fringe of the Promised Land, the Israelites were ready to enter the land. A decision was made to send twelve spies, one from each tribe, to explore the land (Num 13:1).

1. Ten spies reported negatively about the land, and the rest of the Israelites started to grumble and complain

against Moses and Aaron (Num 14:2). Joshua and Caleb, the only two from the twelve spies who gave a positive report, joined Moses and Aaron in trying to convince the people of Israel not to rebel against the Lord (Num 14:5-9).

2. However, the people failed to learn the needed lessons of faith and trust. It seems that fear spread faster than faith. In despair, the congregation blamed Moses, Aaron, and God for a defeat that had not yet occurred.[539] Joshua, on the other hand, was a man of faith, reaffirming the appraisal of the goodness of the land as he declared his complete trust in the Lord's ability to defeat Israel's enemies and deliver the land and its people into their hands.[540]

H. When the time came for Moses to hand over the responsibility of leading the Israelites over to Joshua, Moses encouraged Joshua with these words:

1. "You have seen with your own eyes all that the LORD your God has done to these two kings. The LORD will do the same to all the kingdoms over there where you are going. Do not be afraid of them; the LORD your God himself will fight for you" (Deut 3:21-22).

I. As Moses prepares to transition the nation of Israel from his leadership to Joshua's, he recites a previous victory to remind and encourage Joshua in what God has done and what He has promised.[541]

1. Moses is obeying God's command to encourage Joshua; "Your assistant, Joshua son of Nun, will enter it. Encourage him, because he will lead Israel to inherit it" (Deut 1:38).

2. Later in chapter 3 of Deuteronomy, the Lord tells Moses again to encourage Joshua: "Commission Joshua, and encourage and strengthen him, for he will lead this people across and will cause them to inherit the land that you will see" (Deut 3:28).

J. Unfortunately, Joshua does not follow the same pattern of mentoring someone to follow in his footsteps.

   1. When Joshua reached the end of his life, he had not finished the task of fully taking possession of the Promised Land. The cultural project is now summarized, "Israel served the LORD throughout the lifetime of Joshua and of the elders who outlived him and who had experienced everything the LORD had done for Israel" (Josh 24:31).

   2. Joshua's epitaph: Israel served the Lord no further than the elders who had served with Joshua.[542] Once the elders all passed then, "another generation grew up, who knew neither the LORD nor what he had done for Israel" (Judg 2:10).

III. **Israel's Remaining History**
Israel's history from this point was marked with some amazing acts of trust in God as well as some accounts that are not completely understood today. And yet, from Genesis 12 to Malachi 4, this unfolding cultural project is a record of Israel's education in faith.

   A. Though the Old Testament is filled with some of the most amazing and inspiring stories, there is this lingering realization that continually emerges and lurks under the surface of Israel's history. It is found in Judges, "After that whole generation had been gathered to their fathers, another generation grew up, who knew neither the LORD nor what he had done for Israel" (Judg 2:10). Though Israel had some astonishing highs, the Old Testament constantly presents this reality that exists in humanity, a turning or drifting from the Lord that could leave humanity in a state of hopelessness.

   B. However, the Old Testament is laced with prophetic hope. From Genesis to Malachi, *Yahweh* provided hope that One who could help all of humanity was coming. When recounting the travels of Israel, Moses declared:

1. "The LORD your God will raise up for you a prophet like me from among your own brothers. You must listen to him. For this is what you asked of the LORD your God at Horeb on the day of the assembly when you said, 'Let us not hear the voice of the LORD our God nor see this great fire anymore, or we will die.' The LORD said to me: 'What they say is good. I will raise up for them a prophet like you from among their brothers; I will put my words in his mouth, and he will tell them everything I command him'" (Deut 18:15-18).
   C. Jesus is the turning point in history, fulfilling God's original purposes which He spoke to Abraham, "all peoples on earth will be blessed through you" (Gen 12:3). It would not be just a single peculiar people, but now people drawn from every tribe and nation will be "a chosen people, a royal priesthood, a holy nation, a people belonging to God, that you may declare the praises of him who called you out of darkness into his wonderful light" (1 Pet 2:9). Jesus will be the most significant culture maker in the history of humankind.

If there was one idea or principle you think is important, what would that be?

Seventh Session

"He decreed statutes for Jacob and established the law in Israel, which he commanded our forefathers to teach their children, so the next generation would know them, even the children yet to be born, and they in turn would tell their children" (Ps 78:5-6).

Though the Old Testament is filled with some of the most amazing and inspiring stories, there is this lingering realization that continually emerges and lurks under the surface of Israel's history. It is found in Judges, "After that whole generation had been gathered to their fathers, another generation grew up, who knew neither the LORD nor what he had done for Israel" (Judg 2:10).

Facilitator's Guide

However, the Old Testament is laced with prophetic hope. From Genesis to Malachi, *Yahweh* provided hope that One who could help all of humanity was coming. When recounting the travels of Israel, Moses declared,

> The LORD your God will raise up for you a prophet like me from among your own brothers. You must listen to him. For this is what you asked of the LORD your God at Horeb on the day of the assembly when you said, "Let us not hear the voice of the LORD our God nor see this great fire anymore, or we will die." The LORD said to me: "What they say is good. I will raise up for them a prophet like you from among their brothers; I will put my words in his mouth, and he will tell them everything I command him" (Deut 18:15-18).

I. Jesus, Culture Maker

Jesus is the turning point in history, fulfilling God's original purposes He spoke to Abraham, "all peoples on earth will be blessed through you" (Gen 12:3). It would not be just a single peculiar people but now people drawn from every tribe and nation that will be "a chosen people, a royal priesthood, a holy nation, a people belonging to God, that you may declare the praises of him who called you out of darkness into his wonderful light" (1 Pet 2:9). Jesus will be the most significant culture maker in the history of humankind.

   A. Out of the four biographers of Jesus's life, two include genealogies. Matthew traces Jesus's lineage back to Abraham, which is significant. "Genealogies assert that the story being told is not simply a timeless myth, it is anchored in a particular group of people in a particular place."[543]

   1. Matthew boldly and abruptly states his purpose, "A record of the genealogy of Jesus Christ the son of David, the son of Abraham" (Matt 1:1).

   2. Matthew highlights Jesus's continuity with David, the king of messianic promise and Israel's royal house and links Jesus with Abraham, the father and founding ancestor.[544]

   B. Luke postpones his genealogy until he has told about

Jesus's miraculous conception, His birth, which included the spiritual activity at His dedication (Luke 2:25-38), and His childhood.[545] Then Luke starts Jesus's genealogy with this striking statement, "He was the son, so it was thought, of Joseph, the son of Heli" (Luke 3:23).

1. This may seem like a strange way to begin a genealogy, but Luke had already taken the time to tell of Jesus's miraculous conception in great detail. Luke is making it clear that Joseph is not Jesus's biological father.[546] Luke's genealogy accomplishes two things.

2. First, Luke's genealogy clearly leads the reader to the conclusion that Jesus is "the son of God" (Luke 3:38).

3. Second, Luke's genealogy also makes the case that Jesus is fully and completely human; He is the son of David, the son of Abraham, the son of Adam, and the Son of God (Luke 3:31, 34, 38). If Jesus is completely human, then He has a cultural inheritance.

4. This is also the reason Luke goes into great detail to stress Jesus's genealogy, to emphasize the concern with the continuity of culture that exists with Jesus. If Jesus was not a cultural being, then He was not human at all. However, Jesus followed customs and tradi-tions.[547]

5. Luke states, "When he was twelve years old, they went up to the Feast, according to the custom" (Luke 2:42), and "He went to Nazareth, where he had been brought up, and on the Sabbath day he went into the synagogue, as was his custom. And he stood up to read" (Luke 4:16).

II. **Culture Cultivator**

Jesus did not just pass on Israel's culture inheritance, though the early years of His life were spent learning and living the culture of His people. Nor was Jesus absorbing and practicing culture in order to innovate ways to bring himself into conflict with the nation's leaders.

A. Scripture provides very little of Jesus's years of develop-

Facilitator's Guide

ment, just a couple of glimpses that reveal He was discovering His identity and purpose.

1. This is seen when Jesus was twelve years old and His parents left Jerusalem without Him. When Jesus's parents took three days to look for Him, they found Him in the temple. When Jesus was corrected by His earthly parents, He was surprised that Mary and Joseph did not understand that He would not be in His Heavenly Father's house (Luke 2:49).

2. Following this brief revelation of the twelve-year-old Jesus, Luke states, "And Jesus grew in wisdom and stature, and in favor with God and men" (Luke 2:52).

3. Decades later, the Apostle Paul states, "He is the image of the invisible God, the firstborn over all creation. For by him all things were created: things in heaven and on earth, visible and invisible, whether thrones or powers or rulers or authorities; all things were created by him and for him" (Col. 1:15-16).

4. The important idea here is that Jesus lived out His divinity in a normal life as a young Jewish adult in Nazareth. The One who created all of heaven and earth, lived out His early life as an ordinary person, not concealing His divinity.[548]

B. When the time had fully come, Jesus emerges onto the scene to initiate His public ministry (Mark 1:14-15). Jesus did not come to pass on His cultural inheritance nor cultural relevance but to bring something new to our world. He was preoccupied with the cultural and historical questions that concerned the first-century Jews.

1. The Gospel of Mark provides a synopsis of the new that Jesus would bring. "Jesus went into Galilee, proclaiming the good news of God. 'The time has come,' he said. 'The kingdom of God is near. Repent and believe the good news!'" (Mark. 1:14-15).

2. The word Mark uses for *time* in the Greek does not refer to mere sequence of events but a favorable opportunity or significant time, a sense of urgency or appropriate time.[549]

   a) Mark is referencing the appointed time by God, a divinely appointed time for fulfilling His promises. All of the preparation of ancient Israel and John the Baptist were now complete—being fulfilled in Jesus.

C. The something new Jesus was bringing happened to be the major subject of His message, "the kingdom of God was near" (Mark 1:15). To the first-century Jews, that meant that the prediction of a future kingdom, which would throw off all their oppressors, and Israel would rule the nations.

  1. However, Jesus did not mean an earthly kingdom but a spiritual one that was present referring to God's rule, reign, dominion, and sovereignty in the hearts of people.

     a) In addition, Mark pointed to the fact that the reign and rule of God had started to take place in the life and ministry of Jesus Christ.

  2. As a result of this present but mystical kingdom, Mark highlights a distinctive element in Jesus's message to the people; they must believe the gospel.[550]

     a) Here lies a key; "The people were amazed at his teaching, because he taught them as one who had authority, not as the teachers of the law" (Mark 1:22).

     b) The gap between the Rabbis and Jesus did not lie in the subject matter being taught but in His own person. Jesus knew fully that He was the Son.[551]

D. The Gospel of Matthew presents Jesus teaching a radically new way of thinking. The Sermon on the Mount provides the basic principles for living in the kingdom of God or the kingdom of heaven. It is not the wise and talented who share or take possession of the kingdom of heaven but the "poor in spirit" (Matt 5:3).

Facilitator's Guide

1. The GW translation words this verse this way: "Blessed are those who recognize they are spiritually helpless. The kingdom of heaven belongs to them" (Matt 5:3, GW).

2. Jesus is not referring to the physically poor, those who are so impoverished that they may revert to begging to survive.[552] The culture Jesus is creating begins with an improvised spirit, with an understanding that those who are trying to enter the kingdom are spiritually helpless.

E. Jesus's teaching was creative as He established new standards for living in this kingdom. How foreign and culturally challenging were Jesus's teachings as He continued with the Sermon on the Mount.

1. "Blessed are you when people insult you, persecute you and falsely say all kinds of evil against you because of me. Rejoice and be glad, because great is your reward in heaven, for in the same way they persecuted the prophets who were before you" (Matt 5:11-12).

F. Jesus was not just providing some new information when He spoke of the kingdom of God being near. However, the good news He shared was a comprehensive restructuring of the social life that people would live.

G. This restructuring tackled the deeper issues the law could not address. In the Sermon on the Mount, Jesus moved the law's external focus to the internal state of the human heart. It is important to notice that Jesus's "prescription for changing the heart involves changes in culture." Here are a few excerpts from the Sermon on the Mount to highlight this focus on the heart and culture:[553]

1. Matthew 5:20, "For I tell you that unless your righteousness surpasses that of the Pharisees and the teachers of the law, you will certainly not enter the kingdom of heaven."

2. Matthew 5:22, "But I tell you that anyone who is angry with his brother will be subject to judgment. Again, anyone who says to his brother, 'Raca,' is answerable to

the Sanhedrin. But anyone who says, 'You fool!' will be in danger of the fire of hell."

3. Matthew 5:23-24, "Therefore, if you are offering your gift at the altar and there remember that your brother has something against you, leave your gift there in front of the altar. First go and be reconciled to your brother; then come and offer your gift."

4. Matthew 5:28, "But I tell you that anyone who looks at a woman lustfully has already committed adultery with her in his heart."

5. Matthew 5:38-39, "You have heard that it was said, 'Eye for eye, and tooth for tooth.' But I tell you, Do not resist an evil person. If someone strikes you on the right cheek, turn to him the other also."

6. Matthew 5:43-45, "You have heard that it was said, 'Love your neighbor and hate your enemy.' But I tell you: Love your enemies and pray for those who persecute you, that you may be sons of your Father in heaven."

H. Jesus set new standards that were to dictate the kind of life His followers were to demonstrate to their neighbors and enemies. This new social lifestyle would demonstrate what it looks like to live trusting and depending on God.

1. The greatest innovation that Jesus offered was not the alternative culture He proposed but the life He lived out in front of everyone.

2. Coming full circle, what Israel could not accomplish in their original calling, to demonstrate complete dependence on *Yahweh*, Jesus did fulfill. He fully lived a life totally and completely dependent on *Yahweh*, He did not compromise when faced with the cross.

3. Jesus literally turned the other cheek allowing the Roman soldiers to fully abuse and brutally destroy His body. But for the brokenness of culture to be dealt with, Jesus had to accept the calling of the Cross.[554]

I. Jesus's creative cultivation of culture also included reshaping the Passover meal. He reinterpreted the cup and bread to reflect His death.[555]

  1. The bread speaks that the Bread of life was broken in death in order that life could be given to those who were spiritually hungry and in need.

  2. The cup states that Jesus poured out His blood, which is His life, for life is in the blood. That blood cleanses a person and includes a quickening power.[556]

III. **The Cross and Culture**
Long before Jesus was ever crucified, the cross already existed.

  A. To the Romans, the cross was the ultimate statement to the world; this is what happens to anyone who opposes the empire's offer of peace. Rebellion was not tolerated.

   1. Many had died on the cross before Jesus; however, no other human being before or since Jesus's death on the Cross adequately accomplished what He did. Jesus suffered the full weight of humanity's sin and rebellion against God.

   2. The Cross is designed to extinguish life, ending all creativity and any cultivation. Scripture states, "God made him who had no sin to be sin for us" (2 Cor 5:21).

   3. Jesus dying on the Cross for humanity is the complete deliverance from the burden and curse of sin.[557] "The strangest and most wonderful paradox of the biblical story is that its most consequential moment is not an action but a passion, not a doing but a suffering."[558]

  B. The Cross was not only the symbol describing how Jesus died, but Jesus made it clear that all who would follow Him would need to deny themselves and take up their Cross (Matt 16:24; John 10:18; 1 John 3:16). Though the Cross extinguishes all life, creativity, and cultivation[559] according to human understanding, it really sets the platform for the kind of culture the Church needs to exhibit.

1. The Apostle Paul states in Galatians, "I have been crucified with Christ and I no longer live, but Christ lives in me. The life I live in the body, I live by faith in the Son of God, who loved me and gave himself for me" (Gal 2:20).

2. In several of his Epistles, Paul made it clear that a person following Christ was dead to sin with Christ. In Colossians, Paul stated, "For you have died, and your life is hidden with Christ in God" (Col 3:2, ESV).

IV. **The Greatest Cultural Event in History**

As impacting as the Cross is for cultivating culture, it was the Resurrection that was a culture-shaping event.

    A. Resurrection and Culture

1. As a matter of fact, the Resurrection is the most culturally significant event in all of history. It is the Resurrection that has changed more cultures and more people than any other event in history.[560]

2. So powerful was the Resurrection that believers in the first century changed the day they would meet for worship. Instead of only meeting on Saturday, the official Sabbath, they started meeting on Sunday in honor of the Resurrection.

3. That statement may not seem important, but you must understand that the Sabbath was written into the Ten Commandments as well as the story of creation.

4. Within a few years after Jesus's death, there is record of Jewish believers who, in addition to worshiping on the seventh day for Sabbath also worshipped on the first day of the week in honor of the Resurrection. In Acts, it is stated, "On the first day of the week we came together to break bread. Paul spoke to the people…" (Acts 20:7; 1 Cor 16:2).

5. This is the first clear indication that believers had

augmented their Saturday (Sabbath) worship with worship together on the first day of the week. Millions of lives around the world were shaped through this worship on Sunday.

B. The crucifixion and resurrection of Jesus Christ is the culmination of God's culture-rescuing project that began in Genesis 12.

1. Jesus faced the worst that humanity had to throw at Him only to triumph over all, even humankind's sinfulness and rebellion. It was more than just a spiritual triumph; it was also a cultural victory, as well.

2. Jesus's victory over death, hell, and the grave is the pronouncement that the arrival of God's realm of possibility that is His kingdom is made manifested in humanity's cultural structures. Jesus's victory is also the good news that the kingdom of God is available to all peoples of the world.[561]

C. "In the kingdom of God, a new kind of life and a new kind of culture becomes possible, not by abandoning the old but by transforming it. Even the cross, the worst that culture can do, is transformed into a sign of the kingdom of God, the realm of forgiveness, mercy, love, and indestructible life."[562]

D. Beyond Pentecost

1. The story that unfolds in Acts is one about cities. Like bookends, the story begins in Jerusalem and ends in Rome.

2. In between these two bookends are stops along the way touching just about every commercial and political center around the Mediterranean Sea. Almost all the activity of the Gospel moving through the empire took place in urban centers.

3. This means that Acts is also about culture.

Facilitating Change to Reach All Generations

4. It is clear in Acts that God is on the move and He no longer is telling the story in just one culture. The call for salvation is to every person and every cultural group. "Everyone who calls on the name of the Lord will be saved" (Acts 2:21).

5. Yet, the group at the beginning of Acts on the day of Pentecost was entirely Jewish and still identified with the cultural project of Israel (Acts 2:5).[563]

6. However, a shift began with Peter going to Cornelius's house in Acts 10. The moment Peter walked across the threshold of Cornelius's house, the mission of Jesus began to expand beyond the cultural specificity of Israel.[564]

E. The ministry that began in Acts 2 entirely directed to the Jewish people has now shifted by Acts 17 where Paul is speaking to Greeks.

1. Paul tried to relate to the Greeks by preaching a message closer to Peter's sermon in Acts 2 message, which received this response, "'What is this babbler trying to say?' Others remarked, 'He seems to be advocating foreign gods.' They said this because Paul was preaching the good news about Jesus and the resurrection" (Acts 17:18).

   a) Initially, Paul's message was foolish to the Greeks but when Paul met again in the Areopagus, he changed his approach and adjusted the message.

   b) Before meeting these philosophers, Paul had walked through Athens and noticed that the city was full of idols. In the process of touring Athens, Paul found an idol to an unknown god. Paul connected to this group of Greeks by using that idol and began to tell about Him (Acts 17:22-23).

   c) Then Paul defined the Creator God of the Bible: He is the One who created the world and everything in it (Acts 17:24).[565] Paul wisely led his hearers from the beginning of creation to their need to seek this God who sustains everything and everybody, to the resurrection of Jesus from the dead (Acts 17:25-31).

2. A statement Paul makes conveys the importance and necessity of learning to communicate the Good News to all generations. He says, "In the past God overlooked such ignorance, but now he commands all people everywhere to repent" (Acts 17:30).

3. This follows another important statement made by Barnabas and Paul on their first missionary trip. They said, "In past generations He allowed all the nations to go their own way" (Acts 14:16, HCSB).[566]

4. In the past the Lord allowed nations or people groups to go their own way. However, God did not give up on His plan of redemption or His purpose of blessing all the nations of the earth through fruitful seasons of harvest.[567]

F. When Paul and Barnabas return from their first missionary travel, they share with their community of faith in Antioch all that the Lord had accomplished through them.

1. Again, this dynamic team shares an amazing phrase that makes it known that God has provided all of humanity the opportunity for salvation. Paul and Barnabas's testimony was "that God had... opened the door of faith to the Gentiles" (Acts 14:27).

2. The Greek emphasizes that "a door" of faith was opened to the Gentiles, meaning it was a specific door for the rest of humanity.[568]

V. **Conclusion**

What does all this mean for us today, especially in connecting and reaching the younger generations?

A. This is what is happening, a gap that is widening between the generations, a gap between the Christianized worldview and the non-Christian and secular world.[569]

B. America once fostered a culture that was friendly and receptive toward the gospel message but now is drastically turning away from the gospel. Reaching the younger generation involves more than just learning how the Gen Xers, Millennials, and Gen Zs think.

C. There are absolute differences between the generations, but they were not born in a vacuum. The culture of America has been working to inoculate generations against the Bible so that now the church has a crisis and does not fully understand what is happening.[570]

D. Most people within the Boomer and Gen X generation are trying to reach people from their worldview, and they are not relating well.

E. The last examples given from the book of Acts describing the difference between the Acts 2-type culture and the Acts 17-type culture highlight some of the challenges the church is facing.

F. As an example, I am a Boomer, raised under a strong authoritative father who instilled in me that you respect those who are in authority, follow the rules, be faithful to your task, be responsible, no matter what.

   1. So, when my children were born, though I was now a believer in Jesus Christ, I believed that I had the right to tell my children what to do, correct them for their wrong behavior and beliefs. Today, children are being taught secular humanism from an early age and that they have rights. They sometimes interpret these rights to mean that they do not have to listen to their parents. The dynamic of this shift is huge!

G. When I am trying to witness and reach people for Christ, I am from my worldview, speaking my culture with its standards and beliefs, and I am wondering why I am not connecting with the younger generation.

H. This is what has happened overall within the church:

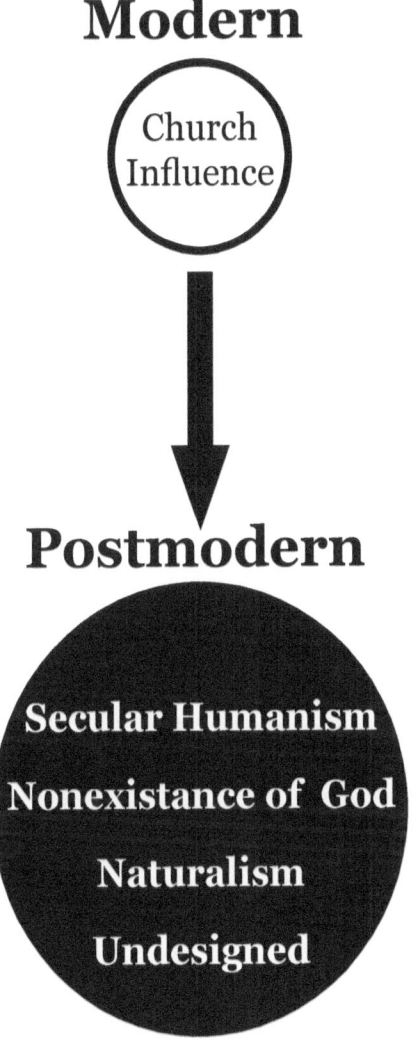

Paul built a bridge to reach those with whom he came in contact (1 Cor 9:19-22). This is the goal, to reach people for Christ.

Chapter 10
Assessing Your Teaching

Should you use the material in this book for a teaching session, you may wish to assess your teaching, to determine whether changes have occurred in the attitudes and understanding of those to whom you are presenting the material. The following provides two methods of doing so, using a pre- and post-assessment instrument and a post-session evaluation form.

Pre- and Post-Assessment Instrument

The following assessment instrument has nineteen questions. You can ask these same questions before and after the teaching session and then compare results.

Table 1. Pre-Post-Assessment Questions

Pre-Assessment

1. Having to take this assessment, are you:
   a. Anxious _____
   b. Calm/peaceful ____
   c. Intimidated _____
   d. Confident ____
   e. Apprehensive ____
   f. Feel nothing ____

2. Do you think understanding the difference between the generations is important?
   a. Yes _____
   b. No _____

3. Is it important to understand how culture affects the church?
   a. Yes _____
   b. No _____

Assessing Your Teaching

4. In which time period were you born?
   a. (1906 – 1945) _____
   b. (1946 – 1964) _____
   c. (1965 – 1980) _____
   d. (1981 – 2000) _____
   e. (2001 – Present) _____

5. Which of the following statements best describes why you attend church? <u>Mark all that apply.</u>
   a. ___ I have attended church all my life, it is a habit.
   b. ___ I want to know God better.
   c. ___ I come to worship God.
   d. ___ I want to meet other people.
   e. ___ I desire to learn what the Bible says
   f. ___ I am curious about God's will for my life.
   g. ___ I would like to serve God and others
   h. ___ I desire to expose my kids to moral and ethical teachings.
   i. ___ I want to get into heaven.
   j. ___ I come because my friends are here.
   k. ___ I am looking to grow spiritually.
   l. ___ I want to help people change the world.
   m. ___ I would like to find peace.

Facilitating Change to Reach All Generations

6. Is your local church [Add Name] effectively serving your generation?

   Yes _____

   No _____

7. How would you describe your position or view of the world?
   a. Conservative _____
   b. Secular _____
   c. Religious _____
   d. Modern _____
   e. Humanistic _____
   f. Biblical _____
   g. Evolutionary _____
   h. Postmodern _____

Assessing Your Teaching

8. Do you consider adults in younger generations as: <u>Mark all that apply</u>.
    a. Uncommitted ____
    b. Committed _____
    c. Disconnected ____
    d. Connected ____
    e. Stable/faithful ____
    f. Technologically savvy ____
    g. Lazy ____
    h. Valuable __
    i. A contributor ____
    j. Confident ____
    k. Expressive ____
    l. Concerned and engaged ____
    m. Unconcerned and disengaging ____

9. Why do you think the younger generations are not connecting to the church today? <u>Mark all that apply</u>.
   a. ___ The Church is irrelevant.
   b. ___ The Church is judgmental and intolerant.
   c. ___ The people are hypocritical.
   d. ___ Too strict.
   e. ___ It does not relate to the younger generation.
   f. ___ The Church talks and uses words not understood today.
   g. ___ The Church is confusing.
   h. ___ All the above
   i. Other _____

10. Which of the following statements/words best describe America's culture? <u>Mark all that apply</u>.
    a. ___ No absolute truth
    b. ___ Truth and error are synonymous.
    c. ___ Self-conceptualization and rationalization replace traditional logic and objectivity.
    d. ___ Traditional authority is false and corrupt.
    e. ___ The fair way to administer goods and services is through collective ownership.
    f. ___ They feel remorse and regret over the unfulfilled promises of religion, science, technology, and government.
    g. ___ Morality is personal.
    h. ___ Globalization supersedes nationalism.
    i. ___ All religions are valid.
    j. ___ Liberal ethics should prevail.
    k. ___ Pro-environmentalism dictates behavior

11. America is an increasingly secular and postmodern culture with a growing number of people knowing little of the traditional church:

    a. True _____

    b. False _____

12. In your opinion, does the Bible communicate culture?

    a. Yes _____

    b. No _____

13. Which one of these words best defines what you believe about how all things were created – universe, earth, all living things, etc.?

    a. Evolution _____

    b. Creationism _____

    c. Naturalism _____

    d. God-guided Evolution _____

    e. Gap Theory _____

    f. Progressive Creationism _____

14. Which item below has the strongest influence in defining who you are?

    a. Your job/profession _____

    b. Theological position _____

    c. Education _____

    d. Achievements _____

    e. Economic status _____

15. If God was developing culture, do you think He would include certain standards, demands, and directives?

    a. Yes _____

    b. No _____

16. What word/s would define God's goal for His culture? <u>Mark all that apply</u>.

    a. Religious _____

    b. Valued possessions _____

    c. Priest _____

    d. Holy _____

    e. Worshippers _____

    f. Covenant Keepers _____

    g. Conformers _____

    h. Cultivators _____

    i. All the above _____

    j. Other _____

17. Did Jesus produce culture?

    a. Yes _____

    b. No _____

18. In your opinion, what is the one thing the Church should be known for?

    a. Giving tithes _____

    b. Worship _____

    c. Preaching _____

    d. Helping the poor _____

    e. Presence _____

    f. Love _____

    g. Grace _____

19. In your understanding of history what is the most significant event that powerfully influenced culture?

    a. WWII _____

    b. The Church _____

    c. Computers _____

    d. The Great Depression _____

    e. Cell phones, Internet, Google _____

    f. The Resurrection _____

    g. Ten Commandments _____

    h. Electricity _____

    i. 9/11 _____

    j. Other _____

The goal of your teaching session will likely be to provide awareness to leaders and influencers, but it may also awaken your congregation to the real challenges involved in reaching all generations. Their thoughts and perspectives will hopefully shift due to your teaching.

Table 2 below contains additional questions you could add to the post-assessment in order to gain further insights.

Table 2. Additional Questions for the Post-Assessment

#	Question

1	Did the material help you understand your generation and some of your behavior better?
	    a. Strongly Agree _____
	    b. Agree _____
	    c. Uncertain _____
	    d. Disagree _____
	    e. Strongly Disagree _____

2	How would you describe your position or view of the world after today's teaching?
	    a. Conservative _____
	    b. Secular _____
	    c. Religious _____
	    d. Modern _____
	    e. Humanistic _____
	    f. Biblical _____
	    g. Evolutionary _____
	    h. Postmodern _____

3	Has your position or view changed toward the adults of the younger generations?
	    a. Yes _____
	    b. Uncertain _____
	    c. No _____

4	If God has created culture, do you think He has a right to set certain standards, demands, and directives? a. Yes _____ b. No _____

Assessing Your Teaching

Presenter's Evaluation Form

Following the seminar, you could also have each participant complete a presenter's evaluation form to evaluate the seminar content and the instructor, as follows:

Subject _____

Presenter _____

	Quantitative Questions:	Excellent 5	Very Good 4	Good 3	Satisfactory 2	Poor 1
1	The objectives of the presentation were clearly defined.					
2	Participation and interaction were encouraged					
3	The topics covered were relevant to me.					
4	The content was organized and easy to follow.					
5	The materials distributed were helpful.					
6	This instructor was knowledgeable about the topics being discussed.					
7	The instructor was well-prepared.					
8	The objectives were met.					
9	The time allotted for this presentation was sufficient.					

	Qualitative Questions:
10	What did you like most about this presentation today?
11	Are there any aspects that could be improved?
12	How do you hope to change any practices, procedures, or behavior as a result of this presentation?

You may find that before the seminar some participants will not have understood the real difference of the generations nor understand how the culture in America had changed and had an effect on everyone, including the church. Hopefully after the seminar participants will express a greater clarity in their understanding of culture, the generations, and what God expects from the believer.

Chapter 11
Benefits to Your Ministry

This material not only can help you discover what may be keeping the younger generation(s) from connecting to your church and provide an understanding of the differences between the generations, but it hopefully also will indicate how culture is shaping everything in today's society. Your leaders and influencers can experience benefits from this teaching on several levels.

1) *Clarity on the differences between the generations.* This information can help people change their posture and attitude toward generations different from themselves.

2) *Changed interactions between those in your congregation and those visiting your church.* People can learn to reach out intentionally to visitors as they have an increased sensitivity of the characteristics that exist with different generations.

3) *Adjusted media presentations so messages communicated relate to all generations.* Such shifts can affect congregant attitudes and behavior and even increase willingness to participate in the ministries of the church.

4) *Adjustments to how your worship team leads worship.* The biblical foundation expressed through the teaching reveals God's desire to build Kingdom culture to be lived out through

the church. The primary distinction of the people of God is His presence. That focus can change how your worship team leads the church in worship as people intentionally strive to be mindful of Christ's abiding presence. This gradual shift of focus on the presence can change the atmosphere of your church!

5) *A change in how people do outreach.* As people's perspectives about the lost or outsiders change, they are more open-minded in their approach to reaching them. Church people should not take offense at unchurched folks' different, wild, or weird views. Instead of just reacting, believers can listen and respond with sensitive answers that demonstrate more of the love of Christ.

6) *Adapting the seminar teaching for a small group format.* Doing this will help you to reach more people for the purpose of shifting the entire congregation toward a Kingdom culture life that exhibits the presence and love of Christ at all levels of living.

Chapter 12
Final Reflections

What We Need to Reach the Generations

A gap is growing between the Christianized worldview and the non-Christian, secular worldview. America once fostered a culture that was friendly and receptive toward the gospel message, but now America is drastically turning away from the gospel and cultural acceptance of Christian tenets. Reaching the generations involves more than just learning how Gen Xers, Millennials, and Gen Zs think. Though differences exist between the generations, none of the generations were born in a vacuum.

From the beginning, God intended a culture that would demonstrate a populace dependent on Him, a people living in a trusted relationship with Him. However, humanity chose a different path and became producers of a counterculture to God's plan. Just as Eve changed her values and beliefs, the younger generation has changed its values and beliefs. Instead of humanity being a cultivator with God, they are now consumers in opposition to God.[571] So what does the Church need as it moves forward in this Kingdom endeavor?

A Strong Theological Foundation

The strength of this book is its biblical-theological foundation, and that same foundation will serve the church's multiplication efforts well in the years to come as it seeks to reach all generations. The Bible's account of creation clarifies that the Lord God intended good for humanity when He placed humans in the Garden He had planted. He provided directives and parameters to aid humanity's productivity and relational interaction. The first three chapters of Genesis reveal the kind of culture God intended. After humanity's failure, God began a new cultural project with Abraham, to be lived out through his descendants. The account of God's supernatural manifestation in Exodus is overwhelming. In it, we can see God's heart for His people. His willingness to disclose himself with such remarkable manifestations of His presence to the nation of Israel is astounding. Exodus offers a vivid revelation of God's love for Israel. God wanted to establish a community of faith with himself at the very center.

As magnificent as those supernatural encounters with *Yahweh* were, the church has a better hope today with a guarantee of a better covenant through Jesus, the ultimate culture cultivator. Since the Day of Pentecost, the Church has been infused with a working of God's power and presence through the Holy Spirit transforming lives and affecting change in culture.

Such a compelling realization can radically transform a believer's perspective on purpose and ministry. Christians need to adjust their lives—more specifically, their attitudes and behaviors—so the gospel can be presented to all generations culturally and the church can connect to people within the community.

Passion

An important key for helping the generations to find Christ is cultivating a passion for them. The need is just as great as ever, if not greater. Media constantly highlights the desperation, hopelessness, and lost-

Final Reflections

ness of humanity with the rise of suicides, the growing opioid epidemic, the intensifying tension among ethnic groups, and the increase in gun violence. The answer is clear; the hope for the generations is in the life-changing power of God's Word and the Holy Spirit. The Lord is the only One who has the ability to soothe the heart searching for hope and meaning. You will need to ask God for a greater passion to serve as a channel of hope.

Empowerment of the Holy Spirit

As you proceed through the teaching materials in this book, you will need more than a passion for reaching the generations and discovering answers that can address the personal issues of your church. You will need to realize the critical role of relying on the Holy Spirit and the part He plays in implementing the solutions presented in this book. God's heart is for the lost, and the Holy Spirit will communicate the Father's concern to those seeking Him for answers.

Sometimes we find ourselves bogged down in the sea of information and may feel lost and overwhelmed about the direction to take. The road can become quite muddled and unclear at times. Thank God for the presence and help of the Holy Spirit. In those moments of feeling overwhelmed, you can call out for the Holy Spirit's help to provide clarity. His faithfulness to respond in those moments of your heartfelt cry for help is truly humbling. The precious Holy Spirit will come in those moments, clearing the confusion, removing the fog, refocusing your vision, and providing a clear path of direction like a lighthouse in bad weather leading ships to safety. He will provide insight and revelation, reminding you of information you've previously read. The Spirit of God will be a great encouragement and aid to you through difficult moments as you strive to walk out your calling and Kingdom vision.

Cultivating a New Culture

Reaching all generations will involve your church understanding that culture has changed and continues to change. The church not only needs to understand culture, but it also needs to cultivate a culture that generates an atmosphere where people can connect with and experience *Yahweh*.

The postmodern, secular humanistic culture of America focuses on humanity's weaknesses as priority. This means that culture is feeding people what they want. The church does not understand the importance of culture. This misunderstanding places the church at odds with not only people's beliefs and values but also what is really their feeding tube. If the culture of the church is not stronger than what the world is feeding the unsaved, then newcomers will not stay. What follows are some practical ways your church can cultivate a new culture:

First, reaching the generations calls for a willingness to conquer the consistent stereotyping on both sides of the church walls. Individuals who live outside the church walls have just as much to overcome as the regular church attenders do. The point here is twofold: one, the outsiders, lost, or unsaved, whatever title the church wishes to place on them, are not going to work at overcoming their preconceived ideas of the church. These individuals see the church as irrelevant to the needs of their lives. Two, it appears that the church seems confused about its understanding of the concept of the people who are unsaved. Some believers assume the unsaved should be willing to change their perception of the church because they should recognize that believers are trying to help them. Another way to say this is believers are expecting unsaved people to act like they are saved, even though they are not.

Second, church folks must be willing to navigate change. At different times in this journey, I have discussed the change in America's culture and some of my finds with other people. Some responded with silence upon hearing the information on cultural shift. Those who were silent maintained an attitude of looking at church with goggles of the past. They interpret the present in light of the past, and they resist information that challenges their paradigm. To create a new culture, one must be willing to navigate change.

Third, instead of looking at the differences that exist between the generations as barriers, the church can see them as strengths that can be used for building strong relationships. Learning not only the strengths but even the weaknesses of each group yields opportunity for building connecting points. A prerequisite to this involves letting go of preconceived ideas one may have of a different generation.

Fourth, the church needs to understand the power of culture. Culture is about people. The postmodern, secular humanistic culture of America focuses on humanity's weaknesses as priority. In other words, culture is feeding the people what they want. The church does not understand how important culture is. If the culture of the church is not strong enough to supplement newcomers with values and purpose that address their needs, they will leave.

Fifth, the church needs to learn the difference between an Acts 2 and an Acts 17 church. An Acts 2 church is not only about the baptism in the Holy Spirit, but also refers to understanding the people the church is trying to reach. Peter preached to a crowd of Jewish people (in Acts 2) who understood his sermon's content. When Paul preached at the Areopagus, he changed his approach and message. Paul started with an idol, "To an Unknown God" (Acts 17:23) and then led his listeners to the God of creation before working his way to Jesus and His resurrection. The church needs to know its audience and the knowledge and backdrop that they are coming from in order to communicate the gospel contextually.

Your church has remarkable opportunities to reach its community for Christ. Instead of seeing generational differences, cultural shifts, and different kinds of people as barriers, the church can turn each of these challenges into possible connecting points for reaching the lost.

About the Author

James W. Wickham and his wife, Isla, reside in beautiful Southern Maryland, about an hour and half from Washington, D.C.

In July of 1986, they planted Living Word Community Church, which they still pastor. They led Living Word from its infancy, through the several stages of growth. Presently they have their own building, with plans of future growth and expansion. As teachers of the Word of God, both James and Isla are passionate about people experiencing the transforming power of Christ's love and the presence of God.

For almost forty years, James has filled various levels of leadership positions for the Assemblies of God Potomac District Ministry Network. For over 20 years, he has served on the board of a local Crisis Pregnancy Center.

In addition to the position of pastor, counselor, mentor, and coach, he holds B.Th., B.A., M.A., and D.Min. degrees.

James and Isla have three grown married children with eight grandchildren.

Endnotes

1   J. R. Woodward. *Creating A Missional Culture: Equipping the Church for the Sake of the World* (Downers Grove, IL: InterVarsity Press, 2012), 55.

2   This working definition for culture is mine, developed from the aggregate of resources on culture.

3   Andy Crouch, *Culture Making: Recovering Our Creative Calling* (Downers Grove, IL: InterVarsity Press, 2008), 23.

4   David Kinnaman and Gabe Lyons, *unChristian: What a New Generation Really Thinks about Christianity ...and Why It Matters* (Grand Rapids, MI: Baker Books, 2012), 27-28.

5   Frank Viola, *Reimaging Church: Pursuing the Dream of Organic Christianity* (Colorado Springs, CO: David C. Cook, 2008), 65.

6   All Scripture quotations, unless otherwise noted, are from the New International Version.

7   Stanley M. Horton, *Genesis*, vol. 1 of *The Complete Biblical Library*, ed. Thoralf Gilbrant, Gregory A. Lint, and Stanley M. Horton (Springfield, MO: World Library Press Inc., 1994), 21.

8   Crouch, *Culture Making*, 22-23.

9   Henry M. Morris, *The Genesis Record: A Scientific and Devotional Commentary on the Book of Beginnings* (San Diego, CA: Creation-Life Publishers, 1976), 90-91.

10   Gordon Fee and Douglas Stuart, *How to Read the Bible Book by Book: A Guided Tour* (Indianapolis: Sure Foundation, 1964), 15.

11   Crouch, *Culture Making*, 21, 108.

12   Horton, *Genesis*, vol. 1 of *The Complete Biblical Library*, 29.

13   Crouch, *Culture Making*, 23.

14   Ibid., 23.

15   Ibid., 73-74.

16   Ibid., 24.

17   Horton, *Genesis*, vol. 1 of *The Complete Biblical Library*, 29.

18   Christopher J. H. Wright, *The Mission of God: Unlocking the Bible's Grand Narrative* (Downers Grove, IL: InterVarsity Press, 2006), 65.

19   Crouch, *Culture Making*, 35.

20   Horton, *Genesis*, vol. 1 of *The Complete Biblical Library*, 35.

21   Ibid., 35.

22   Crouch, *Culture Making*, 113.

23   Ibid., 114.

24   Horton, *Genesis*, vol. 1 of *The Complete Biblical Library*, 31.

25   L. H. Osborn, "Creation," in *New Dictionary of Biblical Theology: Exploring the Unity & Diversity of Scripture*, ed. T. Desmond Alexander, Brian S. Rosner, D. A. Carson, and Graeme Goldsworthy (Downers Grove, IL: InterVarsity Press, 2000), 432.

26   Neil Anderson. *Victory over the Darkness: Realizing the Power of Your Identity in Christ* (Ventura, CA: Regal Books, 2000), 32-33.

27   Bruce R. Marino, *The Origin, Nature, and Consequences of Sin. Systematic Theology*, ed. Stanley M. Horton (Springfield, MO: Logion Press, 2002), 260.

28   William C. Williams and Stanley M. Horton, eds. *They Spoke from God: A Survey of the Old Testament* (Springfield, MO: Gospel Publishing House, 2003), 102.

29   Ibid., 107.

30   Ibid.

31   Horton, *Genesis*, vol. 1 of *The Complete Biblical Library*, 37.

32   Williams and Horton, *They Spoke from God*, 107.

33   Crouch, *Culture Making*, 115.

End Notes

34   Henry C. Thiessen, *Lectures in Systematic Theology* (Grand Rapids: William B. Eerdmans Publishing Company, 2006), 163.

35   Anderson, *Victory over the Darkness*, 36.

36   Williams and Horton, *They Spoke from God*, 113.

37   T. D. Alexander, "Abraham," in *New Dictionary of Biblical Theology: Exploring the Unity & Diversity of Scripture*, ed. T. Desmond Alexander, Brian S. Rosner, D. A. Carson, and Graeme Goldsworthy (Downers Grove, IL: InterVarsity Press, 2000), 367.

38   Crouch, *Culture Making*, 126.

39   Ibid.

40   Anderson, *Victory over the Darkness*, 24.

41   Crouch, *Culture Making*, 127.

42   Old Testament Chronology, *The Holy Bible: New International Version, Life in the Spirit Study Bible* (Grand Rapids: Zondervan, 2003), Frontmatter.

43   Robert Lewis and Wayne Cordeiro, *Culture Shift: Transforming Your Church from the Inside Out* (San Francisco, CA: Jossey-Bass, 2005), 18.

44   Stanley M. Horton, *Revelation*, vol. 10 of *The Complete Biblical Library*, ed. Ralph W. Harris, Stanley M. Horton, and Gayle Garrity Seaver (Springfield, IL: World Library Press, Inc., 1990), 25.

45   John F. Walvoord and Ray B. Zuck, eds. *The Bible Knowledge Commentary: The Old Testament Edition*, Scripture Press Publications, Inc., licensed by Victor Books Database, 2014, WORDsearch Bible, CROSS e-book, 111.

46   Thiessen, *Lectures in Systematic Theology*, 86-87, 109.

47   Iain D. Campbell, *Opening up Exodus*. Opening Up Commentary (Leominster: Day One Publications, 2006), 32, Logos Bible Software.

48   Thiessen, *Lectures in Systematic Theology*, 84.

49   Douglas K. Stuart, *Exodus*, The New American Commentary, vol. 2 (Nashville: Broadman & Holman Publishers, 2006), 114, Logos Bible Software.

50   John F. Walvoord and Ray B. Zuck, eds., *The Bible Knowledge Commentary: The Old Testament Edition* (Scripture Press Publications, Inc. Licensed by Victor Books Database, 1985, 2014), 111, WORDsearch Bible, CROSS e-book.

51   J. R. Dummelow, *A Commentary on the Holy Bible: The One Volume Bible Commentary* (New York: The MacMillan Company, 1909), 51, WORDsearch Bible, CROSS e-book.

52   Robert Jamieson, A. R. Fausset, and David Brown, *Commentary Critical and Explanatory on the Whole Bible* (Oak Harbor, WA: Logos Research Systems, Inc., 1997), Logos Bible Software.

53   Crouch, *Add Short Title*, 126.

54   Lewis and Cordeiro, *Add Short Title*, 18.

55   Gleason L. Archer, *Exodus*, vol. 2 of *The Complete Biblical Library*, ed. Thoralf Gilbrant, and Gregory A. Lint (Springfield, MO: World Library Press Inc., 1996), 31-33.

56   John Peter Lange, Philip Schaff, and Charles M. Mead, *A Commentary on the Holy Scriptures: Exodus* (Bellingham, WA: Logos Bible Software, 2008), Logos Bible Software.

57   Stuart, *Exodus*, 114, Logos Bible Software.

58   Adam Clarke, Adam Clarke's Commentary (New York: Abingdon-Cokesbury Press, 1826), WORDsearch Bible, CROSS e-book.

59   Carl Friedrich Keil, and Franz Delitzsch. *Commentary on the Old Testament* (Peabody, MA: Hendrickson, 1996), Logos Bible Software.

60   Lewis and Corderio, *Culture Shift*, 20.

61   Stuart, *Exodus*, 118, Logos Bible Software.

62   Irving L. Jenson, *Exodus: A Self-Study Guide* (Chicago, IL: Moody Bible Institute, 1967), 24.

63   Stuart, *Exodus*, 118, Logos Bible Software.

64   Walvoord and Zuck, *The Bible Knowledge Commentary*, 112.

65   *Nun-Ayin*, vol. 20 of *The Old Testament Hebrew-English Dictionary*,

End Notes

The Complete Biblical Library, ed. Thoralf Gilbrant, Gregory A. Lint (Springfield, MO: World Library Press Inc., 1999), 340-344.

66   Walvoord and Zuck, *The Bible Knowledge Commentary*, 112.

67   Archer, *Exodus*, vol.2 of *The Complete Biblical Library*, 35.

68   Stuart, *Exodus*, 113-14, Logos Bible Software.

69   George Wagner, *Practical Truths from Israel's Wanderings* (Grand Rapids, MI: Kregel Publications, 1982), 10.

70   Andrew Murray, *The Power of the Blood of Jesus* (New Kensington, PA: Whitaker House, 2004), 9.

71   Horton, *Genesis*, vol. 1 of *The Complete Biblical Library*, 41.

72   Murray, *The Power of the Blood of Jesus*, 20.

73   Crouch, *Culture Making*, 127.

74   Ibid.

75   Archer, *Exodus*, vol.2 of *The Complete Biblical Library*, 199.

76   Ibid., 201.

77   Archer, *Exodus*, vol.2 of *The Complete Biblical Library*, 199.

78   Stuart, *Exodus*, 445, Logos Bible Software.

79   Ibid., 446-447, Logos Bible Software.

80   Ibid., 469.

81   Ibid.

82   Allen Ross, and John N. Oswalt. *Cornerstone Biblical Commentary: Genesis, Exodus*. Vol. 1. Carol Stream, IL: Tyndale House Publishers, 2008. Logos Bible Software.

83   Stuart, *Exodus*, 471. Logos Bible Software.

84   Crouch, *Culture Making*, 130.

85   J. B. Green, "Grace," in *New Dictionary of Biblical Theology: Exploring the Unity & Diversity of Scripture*, ed. T. Desmond Alexander, Brian S. Rosner, D.A. Carson, and Graeme Goldsworthy (Downers Grove, IL: InterVarsity Press, 2000), 524-525.

86   Archer, *Exodus*, vol. 2 of *The Complete Biblical Library*, 35.

87   *The Holy Bible: God's Word, Today's Bible Translation That Means What It Says* (Grand Rapids, MI: World Publishing, 1995).

88   Archer, *Exodus*, vol. 2 of *The Complete Biblical Library*, 185.

89   Dummelow, *A Commentary on the Holy Bible*, 65.

90   Walvoord and Zuck, *The Bible Knowledge Commentary*, 146.

91   Archer, *Exodus*, vol. 2 of *The Complete Biblical Library*, 461.

92   Walvoord and Zuck, *The Bible Knowledge Commentary*, 231.

93   Samuel J. Schultz, *Deuteronomy: The Gospel of Love* (Chicago, IL: Moody Press, 1971), 30.

94   Adam Clarke, *Adam Clarke's Commentary* (New York: Abingdon-Cokesbury Press, 1826), accessed September 8, 2018, WORDsearch Bible, CROSS e-book.

95   Crouch, *Culture Making*, 132.

96   Crouch, *Cultural Making*, 125.

97   French L. Arrington and Roger Stronstad, eds., *Life in the Spirit New Testament Commentary* (Tulsa, OK: Empowered Life Academic, 2017), 154.

98   Crouch, *Cultural Making*, 135.

99   Arrington and Stronstad, *Life in the Spirit New Testament Commentary*, 464.

100   Crouch, *Cultural Making*, 135.

101   Ibid., 136.

102   Zeta-Kappa, Word numbers 2176-2947, vol. 13 of *The New Testament*

End Notes

Greek-English Dictionary, The Complete Biblical Library, ed. Thoralf Gilbrant, Ralph W. Harris, Stanley M. Horton, and Denis W. Vineyard (Springfield, MO: The Complete Biblical Library, 1990), 213.

103   James A. Brooks, *The New American Commentary: Mark*, vol. 23 (Nashville: Broadman & Holman Publishers, 1991), 47, Logos Bible Software.

104   Robert W. Herron, Jr., Vernon D. Doerksen, and Opal L.S. Reddin, *Mark*, vol. 3 of *The Complete Biblical Library*, ed. Thoralf Gilbrant, Ralph W. Harris, and Tor Inge Gilbrant, (Springfield, MO: World Library Press Inc., 1988), 31.

105   Stanley M. Horton, *Matthew*, vol. 2 of *The Complete Biblical Library*, ed. Thoralf Gilbrant, Ralph W. Harris, and Tor Inge Gilbrant, (Springfield, MO: World Library Press Inc., 1989), 75.

106   Crouch, *Culture Making*, 138.

107   Ibid., 139.

108   Ibid., 139-140.

109   Herron, Jr., Doerksen, and Reddin, *Mark*, vol. 3 of *The Complete Biblical Library*, 391.

110   Myer Pearlman, *Knowing the Doctrines of the Bible* (Springfield, MO: Gospel Publishing House, 2017), 357.

111   Andrew Murray, *The Secret of The Cross* (Seattle, WA: Amazon Digital Services LLC.), 33, Kindle.

112   Crouch, *Culture Making*, 142.

113   Ibid., 141.

114   Murray, *The Secret of The Cross*, 51, Kindle.

115   Crouch, *Culture Making*, 143.

116   Stanley M. Horton, *Acts* (Springfield, MO: Logion Press, 2001), 335.

117   Myles Munroe, *Rediscovering the Kingdom: Ancient Hope for Our 21st Century World* (Shippensburg, PA: Destiny Image, Publishers, Inc., 2004), 100.

118   Crouch, *Culture Making*, 146.

119   Ibid., 147.

120   Ken Ham, *Gospel Reset* (Green Forest, AR: Master Books, 2018), 48-49.

121   Crouch, *Culture Making*, 150.

122   Ham, *Gospel Reset*, 94.

123   Stanley M. Horton, *Acts*, vol. 6 of *The Complete Biblical Library*, ed. Thoralf Gilbrant, Ralph W. Harris, and Tor Inge Gilbrant (Springfield, MO: World Library Press, 1991), 345.

124   Horton, *Acts*, vol. 6 of *The Complete Biblical Library*, 353.

125   Crouch, 114.

126   Ham, *Gospel Reset*, 105.

127   Ibid., 106, 108.

128   John Drane, *The McDonaldization of the Church: Consumer Culture and the Church's Future* (Macon, GA: Smyth & Helwys Publishing Inc., 2001), 4.

129   David W. Henderson, *Culture Shift: Communicating God's Truth to Our Changing World* (Grand Rapids, MI: Baker Books, 1999), 10.

130   John Drane, *After McDonaldization: Mission, Ministry, and Christian Discipleship in an Age of Uncertainty* (Grand Rapids, MI: Baker Academic, 2008), 42.

131   David Kinnaman and Gabe Lyons, *unChristian: What a New Generation Really Thinks about Christianity ... and Why It Matters* (Grand Rapids, MI: Baker Books, 2007), 27.

132   Kinnaman and Lyons, *unChristian*, 24.

133   Edward H. Hammett, *Reaching People under Thirty While Keeping People over Sixty: Creating Community across Generations,* The Columbia Partnership Leadership Series (Danvers, MA: TCP, 2015), 1.

134   Ibid., 70.

135   Hammett, *Reaching People under Thirty While Keeping People over Sixty*, 19-20.

End Notes

136   Ibid., 19.

137   Edward H. Hammett, *Spiritual Leadership in a Secular Age: Building Bridges Instead of Barriers* (St. Louis, MO: Chalice Press, 2005), 10.

138   Ibid.

139   Kinnaman and Lyons, *unChristian*, 27.

140   Ibid., 31.

141   Darwin Glassford, *The Church of All Ages*, ed. Howard Vanderwell (Herndon, VA: The Alban Institute, 2008), 71.

142   Kim Ann Zimmermann, "American Culture: Traditions and Customs of the United States," Live Science, accessed June 11, 2018, https://www.livescience.com/28945-american-culture.html.

143   Diane J. Chandler, *Christian Spiritual Formation: An Integrating Approach for Personal and Relational Wholeness* (Downers Grove, IL: IVP Academic, 2014), 123.

144   Texas A&M University, "Definition of Culture," People.tamu.edu, accessed May 26, 2018, http://people.tamu.edu/~i-choudhury//culture.html.

145   Ibid.

146   Ibid.

147   Ibid.

148   Anna Katrina Davey, "*Cultural Confidence: The Art of Global Success*," Cultural Confidence, accessed May 26, 2018, http://culturalconfidence.com/the-meaning-of-culture-by-anna-katrina-davey/.

149   Soong-Chan Rah, *The Next Evangelicalism: Freeing the Church from Western Cultural Captivity* (Downers Grove, IL: IVP Books, 2009), 98-100.

150   Zimmermann, "*American Culture.*"

151   Drane, *After McDonaldization*, 2.

152   Hammett, *Spiritual Leadership in a Secular Age,* 14.

153   Ibid., 7.

154   Ibid., 68.

155   "Characteristics of Postmodernism," All about Philosophy, accessed May 9, 2018, https://www/allaboutphilosopehy.org/characteristics-of-postmoderism.

156   Ibid.

157   Ibid.

158   Ibid.

159   Ibid.

160   Ibid.

161   Ibid.

162   Ibid.

163   Thom S. Rainer and Jess W Rainer, *The Millennials: Connecting to America's Largest Generation* (Hashville, TN: B&H Books, 2011), 156.

164   Carl F. H. Henry, *Postmodernism: The New Spectre?*, *The Challenge of Postmodernism*, ed. David S. Dockery (Grand Rapids, MI: Baker Academic, 2001), 40.

165   "Characteristics of Postmodernism."

166   Brian Duignan, "Postmodernism," Britannica, accessed May 9, 2018, https://www.britannica.com/topic/postmodernism-philosophy.

167   R. Albert Mohler, Jr., *The Integrity of the Evangelical Tradition and the Challenge of the Postmodern Paradigm*, *The Challenge of Postmodernism*, ed. David S. Dockery (Grand Rapids, MI: Baker Academic, 2001), 54.

168   Ross Parsley, *Messy Church: A Multigenerational Mission for God's Family* (Colorado Springs, CO: David C. Cook, 2012), 124.

169   Hammett, *Spiritual Leadership in a Secular Age*, 5.

170   Ibid.

End Notes

171   Hammett, *Reaching People under Thirty While Keeping People over Sixty*, 7.

172   Hammett, *Spiritual Leadership in a Secular Age*, 5.

173   *Reaching People under Thirty While Keeping People over Sixty*, 19-20.

174   Ibid., 19.

175   "Characteristics of Postmodernism."

176   Haydn Shaw, *Sticking Points: How to Get Four Generations Working Together in the Twelve Places They Come Apart* (Carol Stream, IL: Tyndale House Publishers, Inc. 2013), 52.

177   Gary L. McIntosh, *One Church, Four Generations: Embracing the Great Generational Transition* (Grand Rapids, MI: Baker Books, 2002), 199.

178   Shaw, *Sticking Points*, 19.

179   Ibid.

180   Ibid., 19-20.

181   Ibid., 20.

182   Ibid., 21.

183   Ibid., 24.

184   Ibid., 24.

185   McIntosh, *One Church, Four Generations*, 28.

186   Shaw, *Sticking Points*, 51-52.

187   Ibid., 52.

188   Ibid., 53.

189   Ibid.

190   Jill Novak, "The Six Living Generations in America," University of Phoenix, Texas A&M University, accessed June 11, 2018, http://www.market-

ingteacher.com/the-six-living-generations-in-america.

191   Shaw, *Sticking Points*, 54.

192   Novak, "The Six Living Generations in America."

193   Shaw, *Sticking Points*, 64.

194   Ibid., 65.

195   Ibid., 65-66.

196   Ibid., 66.

197   Ibid., 67.

198   Ibid., 66-67.

199   Novak, "The Six Living Generations in America."

200   Shaw, *Sticking Points*, 67.

201   Ibid., 67-68.

202   Ibid., 69.

203   Ibid.

204   Ibid.

205   Novak, "The Six Living Generations in America."

206   Shaw, *Sticking Points*, 70.

207   Ibid.

208   Ibid.

209   Ibid., 71.

210   Ibid., 72.

211   Amy Henson, *Baby Boomers and Beyond: Tapping the Ministry Talents and Passions of Adults over Fifty*, 2nd ed. (San Francisco, CA: Jossey-Bass, 2010),

End Notes

107.

212   Shaw, *Sticking Points*, 77-78.

213   Novak, "The Six Living Generations in America."

214   Ibid.

215   Shaw, *Sticking Points*, 78-79.

216   Ibid., 78-79.

217   Ibid., 79.

218   Ibid., 79-80.

219   Novak, "The Six Living Generations in America."

220   Shaw, *Sticking Points*, 86.

221   Ibid., 86-87.

222   Novak, "The Six Living Generations in America."

223   Shaw, *Sticking Points*, 94.

224   Novak, "The Six Living Generations in America."

225   Shaw, *Sticking Points*, 93-94.

226   Ibid., 94.

227   Marc Robertson, *Working with Millennials: Using Emotional Intelligence and Strategic Compassion to Motivate the Next Generation of Leaders* (Santa Barbara, CA: ABC-CLIO, 2016), 73.

228   Shaw, *Sticking Points*, 95.

229   Jessica Kreigel, *Unfairly Labeled: How Your Workplace Can Benefit from Ditching Generational Stereotypes* (Hoboken, NJ: John Wiley & Sons, 2016), 71.

230   Shaw, *Sticking Points*, 97.

231 Regina Lutterall and Karen McGrath, *The Millennial Mindset: Unraveling Fat from Fiction* (Lanham, MD: The Rowman & Littlefield Publishing Group, 2016), 143.

232 Shaw, *Sticking Points*, 96.

233 Ibid.

234 Shaw, *Sticking Points*, 96-97.

235 Novak, "The Six Living Generations in America."

236 Marc Robertson, *Working with Millennials: Using Emotional Intelligence and Strategic Compassion to Motivate the Next Generation of Leaders* (Santa Barbara, CA: ABC-CLIO, 2016), ix.

237 Rainer and Rainer, *The Millennials*, 80.

238 Ibid., 81.

239 Novak, "The Six Living Generations in America."

240 Drane, *The McDonaldization of the Church*, 70.

241 Ibid., 70.

242 Ibid., 71.

243 Ibid., 70.

244 Ibid., 71.

245 Merriam-Webster.com, accessed May 18, 2018, https://www.merriam-webster.com/dictionary/hedonist.

246 Drane, *The McDonaldization of the Church*, 14.

247 Ibid., 13-15.

248 Ibid., 77.

249 Ibid., 78-79.

250 Ibid., 80.

251   Ibid.

252   Ibid., 81.

253   Ibid., 82-83.

254   Ibid., 85-86.

255   Ibid., 87.

256   Ibid.

257   Ibid., 87-88.

258   Ibid., 88.

259   Ibid., 89.

260   Ibid., 90.

261   Ibid., 91-92.

262   Ibid., 91.

263   Outsiders are those who are outside of Christianity, the Church, and the Christian faith.

264   Kinnaman and Lyons, *unChristian*, 27.

265   Ibid., 44-45.

266   Ibid., 66-67.

267   Ibid., 27, 90.

268   Ibid., 27-28.

269   Ibid., 152.

270   Ibid., 28.

271   Ibid., 28.

272   Mark Labberton, *Called: The Crisis and Promise of Following Jesus*

Today (Downers Grove, IL: IVP Books, 2014), 25-26.

273   Ibid., 26.

274   Lee Kricher, *For a New Generation: A Practical Guide for Revitalizing Your Church* (Grand Rapids, MI: Zondervan, 2016), 144.

275   Shaw, *Sticking Points*, 17.

276   Ibid., 30.

277   Kricher, *For a Generation*, 144.

278   Anna Liotta, *Unlocking Generational Codes* (Lake Placid, NY: Avivia Publishing, 2012), 24.

279   Shaw, *Sticking Points*, 30

280   Ibid., 108.

281   Ibid., 113.

282   Liotta, *Unlocking Generational Codes*, 25.

283   Ibid., 74.

284   Regina Luttrell and Karen McGrath, *The Millennial Mindset: Unraveling Fact from Fiction* (Lanham, MD: The Rowman & Littlefield Publishing Group, 2016), 42.

285   Shaw, *Sticking Points*, 124-125.

286   Ibid., 132-133.

287   Lauren Stiller Rikleen, *You Raised Us—Now Work with Us: Millennials, Career Success, and Building Strong Workplace Teams* (Chicago, IL: ABA Publishing, 2016), 142.

288   Shaw, *Sticking Points*, 140-141.

289   Ibid., 150.

290   Thom S. Rainer and Jess W. Rainer, *The Millennials: Connecting to America's Largest Generation* (Nashville, TN: B&H Books, 2011), 136.

End Notes

291   Lynne C. Lancaster and David Stillman, *When Generations Collide: Who They Are, Why They Clash. How to Solve the Generational Puzzle at Work* (New York: HarperBusiness, 2002), 141-143.

292   Shaw, *Sticking Points*, 160-161.

293   Ibid., 170-171.

294   Ibid., 182-183.

295   Robertson, *Working with Millennials*, 89-90.

296   Shaw, *Sticking Points*, 190-191.

297   Ibid., 205.

298   Liotta, *Unlocking Generational Codes*, 101.

299   Shaw, *Sticking Points*, 208-209.

300   Lynne C. Lancaster and David Stillman, *When Generations Collide: Who They Are. Why They Clash. How to Solve the Generational Puzzle at Work* (New York: HarperBusiness, 2002), 276.

301   Ibid., 282.

302   Shaw, *Sticking Points*, 225.

303   Robertson, *Working with Millennials*, 64.

304   Shaw, *Sticking Points*, 228.

305   Edward H. Hammett, *Reaching People under Thirty While Keeping People over Sixty: Creating Community across Generations,* The Columbia Partnership Leadership Series (Danvers, MA: TCP, 2015), 19-20.

306   Gary L. McIntosh, *One Church, Four Generations: Embracing the Great Generational Transition* (Grand Rapids, MI: Baker Books, 2002), 28.

307   Hayden Shaw, *Sticking Points: How to Get Four Generations Working Together in the Twelve Place They Come Apart* (Carol Stream, IL: Tyndale House Publishing, 2013), 51-52.

308   Ibid., 52.

Facilitating Change to Reach All Generations

309   Ibid., 53.

310   Ibid.

311   Jill Novak, "*The Six Living Generations in America*," University of Phoenix, Texas A&M University, accessed June 11, 2018, http://www.marketingteacher.com/the-six-living-generations-in-america.

312   Shaw, *Sticking Points*, 54.

313   Novak, "The Six Living Generations in America."

314   Shaw, *Sticking Points*, 64.

315   Ibid., 65.

316   Ibid., 65-66.

317   Ibid., 66.

318   Ibid., 67.

319   Ibid., 66-67.

320   Novak, "The Six Living Generations in America."

321   Shaw, *Sticking Points*, 67.

322   Ibid., 67-68.

323   Ibid., 69.

324   Ibid.

325   Ibid.

326   Novak, "The Six Living Generations in America."

327   Shaw, *Sticking Points*, 70.

328   Ibid.

329   Ibid.

330   Ibid., 71.

331   Ibid., 72.

332   Shaw, *Sticking Points*, 77.

333   Novak, "The Six Living Generations in America."

334   Ibid.

335   Shaw, *Sticking Points*, 78-79.

336   Ibid., 79.

337   Ibid., 79-80.

338   Novak, "The Six Living Generations in America."

339   Shaw, *Sticking Points*, 86.

340   Ibid., 86-87.

341   Novak, "The Six Living Generations in America."

342   Shaw, *Sticking Points*, 94.

343   Novak, "The Six Living Generations in America."

344   Shaw, *Sticking Points*, 93-94.

345   Ibid., 94.

346   Ibid., 95.

347   Ibid., 97.

348   Ibid., 96.

349   Ibid.

350   Ibid., 96-97.

351   Marc Robertson, *Working with Millennials: Using Emotional Intelligence and Strategic Compassion to Motivate the Next Generation of Leader*s

(Santa Barbara, CA: ABC-CLIO, 2016), ix.

352   Novak, "The Six Living Generations in America."

353   Ibid.

354   Ibid.

355   Ibid.

356   Edward H. Hammett, *Reaching People under Thirty While Keeping People over Sixty: Creating Community across Generations,* The Columbia Partnership Leadership Series (Danvers, MA: TCP, 2015), 19-20.

357   Ibid., 19-20.

358   Ibid.

359   Ibid.

360   John Drane, *After McDonaldization: Mission, Ministry, and Christian Discipleship in an Age of Uncertainty* (Grand Rapids, MI: Baker Academic, 2008), 70.

361   Ibid., 71.

362   Ibid., 70.

363   Ibid., 71.

364   Annual Report on The Homeless," Maryland's Interagency Council on Homelessness, accessed December 8, 2017, http://www.dhr.state.md.us/blog/wp-content/uploads/2015/01/Homeless-Services-Annual-Report-2015.

365   Ibid.

366   Merriam-Webster.com, accessed May 18, 2018, https://www.merriam-webster.com/dictionary/hedonist.

367   Drane, *The McDonaldization of the Church*, 14.

368   Ibid.

369   Ibid., 13-14.

370	Ibid.
371	Ibid., 77.
372	Ibid.
373	Ibid.
374	Ibid.
375	Ibid., 78-79.
376	Ibid., 80.
377	Ibid.
378	Ibid.
379	Ibid., 81.
380	Ibid., 82-83.
381	Ibid.
382	Ibid.
383	Ibid.
384	Ibid.
385	Ibid., 85-86.
386	Ibid.
387	Ibid.
388	Ibid., 87.
389	Ibid.
390	Ibid., 87-88.
391	Ibid.

392   Ibid., 89.

393   Ibid., 90.

394   Ibid.

395   Ibid., 91-92.

396   Ibid., 91.

397   Kim Ann Zimmermann, "*American Culture: Traditions and Customs of the United States*," Live Science, accessed June 11, 2018, https://www.livescience.com/28945-american-culture.html.

398   Texas A&M University, "Definition of Culture," People.tamu.edu, accessed May 26, 2018, http://people.tamu.edu/~i-choudhury//culture.html.

399   Ibid.

400   Ibid.

401   Ibid.

402   Ibid.

403   Ibid.

404   Ibid.

405   Ibid.

406   Ibid.

407   Anna Katrina Davey, "*Cultural Confidence: The Art of Global Success*," Cultural Confidence, accessed May 26, 2018, http://culturalconfidence.com/the-meaning-of-culture-by-anna-katrina-davey/.

408   Kim Ann Zimmermann, "*American Culture: Traditions and Customs of the United States*," Live Science, accessed June 11, 2018, https://www.livescience.com/28945-american-culture.html.

409   Ibid.

410   Drane, *After McDonaldization*, 2.

End Notes

411   Edward H. Hammett, *Spiritual Leadership in a Secular Age: Building Bridges Instead of Barriers* (St. Louis, MO: Chalice Press, 2005), 14.

412   Drane, *The McDonaldization of the Church*, 6-7.

413   Ibid., 68.

414   "Characteristics of Postmodernism," All about Philosophy, accessed May 9, 2018, https://www/allaboutphilosopehy.org/characteristics-of-postmoderism.

415   Ibid.

416   Ibid.

417   Ibid.

418   Ibid.

419   Ibid.

420   Ibid.

421   Ibid.

422   Ibid.

423   Brian Duignan, "*Postmodernism*," Britannica, accessed May 9, 2018, https://www.britannica.com/topic/postmodernism-philosophy.

424   Ross Parsley, Messy Church: A Multigenerational Mission for God's Family (Colorado Springs, CO: David C. Cook, 2012), 214.

425   Free Inquiry, "What is Secular Humanism?" accessed October 2, 2018, https://secularhumanism.org/what-is-secular-humanism/.

426   Ibid.

427   Ibid.

428   Merriam-Webster Dictionary accessed October 2, 2018, https://www.merriam-webster.com/dictionary/religion.

429   Free Inquiry, "What is Secular Humanism?" accessed October 2, 2018,

https://secularhumanism.org/what-is-secular-humanism/.

430   Ibid.

431   Ibid.

432   Ibid.

433   Ibid.

434   Ibid.

435   ChristianAnswers.Net, "What is Secular Humanism?" accessed October 2, 2018, http://chriatiananswers.net/q-sum/sum-r002.html.

436   Ibid.

437   Ibid.

438   Ibid.

439   Ibid.

440   George Barna, "Survey Reveals That Fewer Adults Have a Biblical Worldview Now Than Two Years Ago," George Barna, http://www.georgebarna.com/research-flow/2018/10/17/survey-reveals-that-fewer-adults-have-a-biblical-worldview-now-than-two-years-ago, accessed January 17, 2020.

441   Brandon Showalter, "Only 1 in 10 Americans Have Biblical Worldview, Just 4 Percent of Millennials: Barna," The Christian Post, Church Ministries, Tuesday, February 28, 2017, https://www.christianpost.com/news/1-in-10-americans-have-biblical-worldview-just-4-percent-of-millennials-barna.html, accessed January 17, 2020.

442   George Barna, "State of the Bible 2019: Trends in Engagement," https://www.barna.com/research/state-of-the-bible-2019/, accessed January 17, 2020.

443   David Noebel, *Understanding the Times: The Religious Worldviews of Our Day and the Search for Truth* (Eugene, OR: Harvest House Publishers, 1991), 8.

444   Del Tackett, "What's A Christian Worldview?" Focus on The Family, https://www.focusonthefamily.com/faith/whats-a-christian-worldview/, accessed October 2, 2018.

End Notes

445   Ibid.

446   David Noebel, "Understanding Six Worldviews that Rule the World," Tree of Life Blog, August 27, 2009, https://treeoflifeblog.com/2009/08/27/understanding-six-worldviews-that-rule-the-world-david-noebel/, accessed January 17, 2020.

447   Tackett.

448   Ibid.

449   Ibid.

450   Ibid.

451   Ibid.

452   Ibid.

453   Ibid.

454   Ibid.

455   Ibid.

456   Ibid.

457   Ibid.

458   Ibid.

459   Ibid.

460   Ibid.

461   Peterson, Eugene H., ed. *The Message: The Bible in Contemporary Language* Colorado Springs, CO: NavPress, 2002. WORD*search* CROSS e-book.

462   Stanley M. Horton, *Genesis*, vol. 1 of *The Complete Biblical Library*, ed. Thoralf Gilbrant, Gregory A. Lint, and Stanley M. Horton (Springfield, MO: World Library Press Inc., 1994), 21.

463   Andy Crouch, *Culture Making: Recovering Our Creative Calling* (Downers Grove, IL: InterVarsity Press, 2008), 22-23.

464   Ibid.

465   Henry M. Morris, *The Genesis Record: A Scientific and Devotional Commentary on the Book of Beginnings* (San Diego, CA: Creation-Life Publishers, 1976), 90-91.

466   Gordon Fee and Douglas Stuart, *How to Read the Bible Book by Book: A Guided Tour* (Indianapolis: Sure Foundation, 1964), 15.

467   Crouch, *Culture Making*, 21, 108.

468   Ibid., 23.

469   Ibid.

470   Horton, *Genesis*, vol. 1 of *The Complete Biblical Library*, 29.

471   Christopher J. H. Wright, *The Mission of God: Unlocking the Bible's Grand Narrative* (Downers Grove, IL: InterVarsity Press, 2008), 65.

472   Crouch, *Culture Making*, 35.

473   Horton, *Genesis*, vol. 1 of *The Complete Biblical Library*, 35.

474   Ibid., 35.

475   Crouch, *Culture Making*, 113.

476   Ibid., 114.

477   Horton, *Genesis*, vol. 1 of *The Complete Biblical Library*, 31.

478   Neil Anderson. *Victory over the Darkness: Realizing the Power of Your Identity in Christ* (Ventura, CA: Regal Books, 2000), 32-33.

479   William C. Williams and Stanley M. Horton, eds. *They Spoke from God: A Survey of the Old Testament* (Springfield, MO: Gospel Publishing House, 2003), 102.

480   Ibid., 107.

481   Ibid.

482   Horton, *Genesis*, vol. 1 of *The Complete Biblical Library*, 37.

End Notes

483 Williams and Horton, *They Spoke from God*, 107.

484 Crouch, *Culture Making*, 115.

485 Ibid., 115.

486 Ibid.

487 Ibid.

488 Anderson, *Victory over the Darkness*, 36.

489 Williams and Horton, *They Spoke from God*, 113.

490 T. D. Alexander, "Abraham," in *New Dictionary of Biblical Theology: Exploring the Unity & Diversity of Scripture*, ed. T. Desmond Alexander, Brian S. Rosner, D. A. Carson, and Graeme Goldsworthy (Downers Grove, IL: InterVarsity Press, 2000), 367.

491 Crouch, *Culture Making*, 126.

492 Ibid.

493 Anderson, *Victory over the Darkness*, 24.

494 Crouch, *Culture Making*, 127.

495 "Old Testament Chronology," in *The Holy Bible: New International Version, Life in the Spirit Study Bible* (Grand Rapids: Zondervan, 2003), Front-matter.

496 Robert Lewis and Wayne Cordeiro, *Culture Shift: Transforming Your Church from the Inside Out* (San Francisco, CA: Jossey-Bass, 2005), 18.

497 Stanley M. Horton, *Revelation*, vol. 10 of *The Complete Biblical Library*, ed. Ralph W. Harris, Stanley M. Horton, and Gayle Garrity Seaver (Springfield, IL: World Library Press, Inc., 1990), 25.

498 John F. Walvoord and Ray B. Zuck, eds. *The Bible Knowledge Commentary: The Old Testament Edition*, Scripture Press Publications, Inc., licensed by Victor Books Database, 2014, 111, WORDsearch Bible, CROSS e-book.

499 Henry C. Thiessen, *Lectures in Systematic Theology* (Grand Rapids: William B. Eerdmans Publishing Company, 2006), 109.

500 Iain D. Campbell, *Opening up Exodus*. Opening Up Commentary (Leominster: Day One Publications, 2006), 32, Logos Bible Software.

501 Thiessen, *Lectures in Systematic Theology*, 84.

502 Douglas K. Stuart, *Exodus*, The New American Commentary, vol. 2 (Nashville: Broadman & Holman Publishers, 2006), 114, Logos Bible Software.

503 John F. Walvoord and Ray B. Zuck, eds., *The Bible Knowledge Commentary*, 111.

504 J. R. Dummelow, *A Commentary on the Holy Bible: The One Volume Bible Commentary* (New York: The MacMillan Company, 1909), 51, WORDsearch Bible, CROSS e-book.

505 Robert Jamieson, A. R. Fausset, and David Brown, *Commentary Critical and Explanatory on the Whole Bible* (Oak Harbor, WA: Logos Research Systems, Inc., 1997), Logos Bible Software.

506 Crouch, *Culture Making*, 126.

507 Gleason L. Archer, *Exodus*, vol. 2 of *The Complete Biblical Library*, ed. Thoralf Gilbrant, and Gregory A. Lint (Springfield, MO: World Library Press Inc., 1996), 31-33.

508 Stuart, *Exodus*, 114, Logos Bible Software.

509 John Peter Lange, Philip Schaff, and Charles M. Mead, *A Commentary on the Holy Scriptures: Exodus* (Bellingham, WA: Logos Bible Software, 2008), Logos Bible Software.

510 Carl Friedrich Keil, and Franz Delitzsch. *Commentary on the Old Testament* (Peabody, MA: Hendrickson, 1996), Logos Bible Software.

511 Lewis and Corderio, *Culture Shift*, 20.

512 Ibid.

513 Stuart, *Exodus*, 118, Logos Bible Software.

514 Irving L. Jenson, *Exodus: A Self-Study Guide* (Chicago, IL: Moody Bible Institute, 1967), 24.

515 Stuart, *Exodus*, 118, Logos Bible Software.

End Notes

516   Walvoord and Zuck, *The Bible Knowledge Commentary*, 112.

517   *Nun-Ayin*, vol. 20 of *The Old Testament Hebrew-English Dictionary*, The Complete Biblical Library, ed. Thoralf Gilbrant, Gregory A. Lint (Springfield, MO: World Library Press Inc., 1999), 340-344.

518   Walvoord and Zuck, *The Bible Knowledge Commentary*, 112.

519   *The Holy Bible: English Standard Version* Wheaton, IL: Crossway Bibles, 2011. WORD*search* CROSS e-book.

520   Archer, *Exodus*, vol.2 of *The Complete Biblical Library*, 35.

521   Ibid.

522   Stuart, *Exodus*, 113-14, Logos Bible Software.

523   George Wagner, *Practical Truths from Israel's Wanderings* (Grand Rapids, MI: Kregel Publications, 1982), 10.

524   Crouch, *Culture Making*, 127.

525   Archer, *Exodus*, vol.2 of *The Complete Biblical Library*, 199.

526   Ibid., 201.

527   Ibid., 199.

528   Stuart, *Exodus*, 445, Logos Bible Software.

529   Ibid., 446-447, Logos Bible Software.

530   Ibid., 471, Logos Bible Software.

531   Ibid., 469, Logos Bible Software.

532   J. B. Green, "Grace," in *New Dictionary of Biblical Theology: Exploring the Unity & Diversity of Scripture*, ed. T. Desmond Alexander, Brian S. Rosner, D.A. Carson, and Graeme Goldsworthy (Downers Grove, IL: InterVarsity Press, 2000), 524-525.

533   Archer, *Exodus*, vol.2 of *The Complete Biblical Library*, 35.

534   *The Holy Bible: God's Word, Today's Bible Translation That Means*

What It Says (Grand Rapids: World Publishing, 1995).

535   Archer, *Exodus*, vol. 2 of *The Complete Biblical Library*, 185.

536   *The Holy Bible, New Living Translation* Wheaton, IL: Tyndale House Publishers, 2004. WORDsearch CROSS e-book.

537   Dummelow, *A Commentary on the Holy Bible*, 65.

538   Walvoord and Zuck, *The Bible Knowledge Commentary*, 146.

539   Archer, *Exodus*, vol. 2 of *The Complete Biblical Library*, 461.

540   Walvoord and Zuck, *The Bible Knowledge Commentary*, 231.

541   Samuel J. Schultz, *Deuteronomy: The Gospel of Love* (Chicago, IL: Moody Press, 1971), 30.

542   Adam Clarke, *Adam Clarke's Commentary* (New York: Abingdon-Cokesbury Press, 1826), accessed September 8, 2018, WORDsearch Bible, CROSS e-book.

543   Crouch, *Culture Making*, 132.

544   French L. Arrington and Roger Stronstad, eds., *Life in the Spirit New Testament Commentary* (Tulsa, OK: Empowered Life Academic, 2017), 154.

545   Crouch, *Cultural Making*, 135.

546   Arrington and Stronstad, *Life in the Spirit New Testament Commentary*, 464.

547   Crouch, *Cultural Making*, 135.

548   Ibid., 136.

549   *Zeta-Kappa*, Word numbers 2176-2947, vol. 13 of *The New Testament Greek-English Dictionary*, The Complete Biblical Library, ed. Thoralf Gilbrant, Ralph W. Harris, Stanley M. Horton, and Denis W. Vineyard (Springfield, MO: The Complete Biblical Library, 1990), 213.

550   James A. Brooks, *The New American Commentary: Mark*, vol. 23 (Nashville: Broadman & Holman Publishers, 1991), 47, Logos Bible Software.

End Notes

551   Robert W. Herron, Jr., Vernon D. Doerksen, and Opal L.S. Reddin, *Mark*, vol. 3 of *The Complete Biblical Library*, ed. Thoralf Gilbrant, Ralph W. Harris, and Tor Inge Gilbrant, (Springfield, MO: World Library Press Inc., 1988), 31.

552   Stanley M. Horton, Matthew, vol. 2 of *The Complete Biblical Library*, ed. Thoralf Gilbrant, Ralph W. Harris, and Tor Inge Gilbrant, (Springfield, MO: World Library Press Inc., 1989), 75.

553   Crouch, *Culture Making*, 138.

554   Ibid., 139-140.

555   Herron, Jr., Doerksen, and Reddin, *Mark*, vol. 3 of *The Complete Biblical Library*, 391.

556   Myer Pearlman, *Knowing the Doctrines of the Bible* (Springfield, MO: Gospel Publishing House, 2017), 357.

557   Andrew Murray, *The Secret of The Cross* (Seattle, WA: Amazon Digital Services LLC.), 33, Kindle.

558   Crouch, *Culture Making*, 142.

559   Ibid., 141.

560   Ibid., 141.

561   Myles Munroe, *Rediscovering the Kingdom: Ancient Hope For Our 21st Century World* (Shippensburg, PA: Destiny Image, Publishers, Inc., 2004), 100.

562   Crouch, *Culture Making*, 146.

563   Ken Ham, *Gospel Reset* (Green Forest, AR: Master Books, 2018), 48-49.

564   Crouch, *Culture Making*, 150.

565   Ham, *Gospel Reset*, 94.

566   *The Holy Bible: Holman Christian Standard Bible* Nashville: Holman Bible, 1999. WORD*search* CROSS e-book.

567   Stanley M. Horton, *Acts*, vol. 6 of *The Complete Biblical Library*, ed. Thoralf Gilbrant, Ralph W. Harris, and Tor Inge Gilbrant (Springfield, MO: World Library Press, 1991), 345.

568 Horton, *Acts*, vol. 6 of *The Complete Biblical Library*, 353.

569 Ham, *Gospel Reset*, 105.

570 Ibid., 106, 108.

571 Crouch, 114.

www.ingramcontent.com/pod-product-compliance
Lightning Source LLC
Chambersburg PA
CBHW031103080526
44587CB00011B/808